The Law of Redemption

What Must One Do to Go to Heaven?

Kathleen Kaczmarek

Copyright © 2016, Kathleen Kaczmarek

ISBN: 978-1-60383-523-7

Published by:
Holy Fire Publishing

www.ChristianPublish.com

Developmental Editor: Rachel E. Newman

Graphic design, photography and cover concept: Dominic Bard

Printed in the United States of America and the United Kingdom

DEDICATION

Jesus, this book is dedicated to you. I cannot thank you enough for what you have done for me. To think of where I came from and where I am now, I thank you so much that you didn't turn a deaf ear to my cry for help. I thank you that you didn't give up on me. No, instead, you pursued me when I was lost and you came to my rescue. I will be forever grateful that you forgave me of my sins and received me unto yourself again. I love you and you mean everything to me.

TABLE OF CONTENTS

ACKNOWLEDGMENTS

I want to acknowledge you, Paul, for your love and for your support. You believe in me and in the message the Lord has given me. This means so much to me. We both can testify that God was our matchmaker and that He knows what He is doing. You are a tremendous husband to me. Your servant's heart doesn't go unnoticed. Thank you for your faithfulness and for your relentless support. I love you.

I also want to acknowledge you, Rachel. I believe that you were assigned by God to edit this book. I want to thank you for your hard work, your passion, and your dedication to this project. You went above and beyond by praying for this project. I want to acknowledge you and express my sincere thanks to you for your tremendous contribution to this work. No doubt, you really made a great deal of difference in the final product of this book; this book would not be what it is today had it not been for you. Thank you.

Mama and Papa, thank you for giving me life. I love you both. Mama, I want to specifically acknowledge your incredible love and self-denial for us, your children, during your entire life. Everything you have done for us, your children, is absolutely worthy of praise. Merci!

INTRODUCTION

In spite of all this, they sinned still more, for they believed not in (relied not on and adhered not to Him for) His wondrous works. Therefore their days He consumed like a breath [in emptiness, falsity, and futility] and their years in terror and sudden haste. When He slew [some of] them, [the remainder] inquired after Him diligently, and they repented and sincerely sought God [for a time]. And they [earnestly] remembered that God was their Rock, and the Most High God their Redeemer. Nevertheless they flattered Him with their mouths and lied to Him with their tongues. For their hearts were not right or sincere with Him, neither were they faithful and steadfast to His covenant. But He, full of [merciful] compassion, forgave their iniquity and destroyed them not; yes, many a time He turned His anger away and did not stir up all His wrath and indignation. For He [earnestly] remembered that they were but flesh, a wind that goes and does not return. How often they defied and rebelled against Him in the wilderness and grieved Him in the desert!

—Psalm 78:32–40

In 2003, the Lord gave me a dream. In the dream, I was in a valley in the desert. There was sand as far as my eyes could see, and it was a bright, sunny day. Suddenly, at the top of the hill appeared angry people. They were holding weapons of some kind. I don't know how many people there were since, being at a lower altitude, I couldn't see beyond the top of the hill. Their attire and weapons suggested they might have been from Jesus' days, though I couldn't tell for sure. They were tanned from spending much time under the sun.

This is when Jesus appeared nearby them on the right. He was wearing what looked like a white kilt and a white banner crossed over His chest. This banner is what revealed to me who He was: the King. Then, without warning, His wrath came out from within Him as though it exploded from inside of Him to fill the whole universe in a split second; and with a powerful force, it immediately returned inside of Him. He had *once again* held back His judgment. He looked in my direction and said, "Save my people." Then he looked downward with sadness on His face, turned around, and began to walk away. When I realized He was going to leave me with these angry people, I cried, "No! Don't leave me! I can't do this without you!" But no sooner had I pleaded with Him not to leave me than I remembered that the Holy Spirit would be with me. Boldness came over me as I felt I had to convince these angry people they needed to believe.

For the longest time after this dream, I wondered how it was that God's people needed to be saved, and I questioned if I had heard correctly. Did He really say, "Save my people"? Weren't God's people saved already? Maybe He said, "Save people" or "Save the people" or "Save these people"? It just didn't add up. It wasn't until, I would say, 2011, when I had become deeply entrenched in legalism, that I began to understand what Jesus meant when He told me these very sobering words. The message finally made sense within the context He spoke it; angry people, weapons . . . they do make me think a lot of the Pharisees. After all, it was the Pharisees that sought to kill Jesus.

Little did I know when I received the dream that the day would come when I myself would need to be saved. Saved from what? Saved from the grip of legalism and its end, the wrath of the Lamb, if I kept it up and continued down that path.

I am beyond myself when I think that Jesus, who hated the hypocrisy of the Pharisees more than anything else, loved me so much while I had become such a legalist myself. This is what touched me the most: to have Jesus, who hates with a passion the deeds of the legalist, stop for me and pursue me until I returned home. He not only sought me, but, once He found me, He also lovingly and without condemnation restored me back to a place where we could enjoy communion and fellowship again. This entire process took time. But His hot pursuit of me and His readiness to help me when I was in my deepest despair are what touched my heart the most about Him. I began to realize Jesus is not this impatient, angry, harsh, and hard-to-please Lord that legalism makes Him to be. And the purpose of this book is to expose legalism, to teach about the finished work of the cross and what it means to us, and to help you know who the real Jesus is. Legalism portrays Jesus as someone He is not, as another Jesus. In other words, legalism teaches another gospel.

I remember reading a book on the topic of legalism during my recovery from legalism and literally hugging the book and kissing it with tears in my eyes because of the love that was expressed for me and people like me. I had felt so ugly inside, and I thought I deserved to be condemned by God and by men. It seemed as though I had sinned the worst sin of all, but I also wanted to come out of it.

But how did it all work? If the Bible said we were justified by faith alone (Romans 3:28), but it also said without holiness no man shall see God (Hebrews 12:14), then I needed to understand how the two statements worked together and how they were, in fact, not contradicting each other, especially when I was painfully aware my performance was far from perfect.

If you are at all like I was, your imperfections scare you a lot. However, if God transforms us from glory to glory just like the Bible says (2 Cor. 3:18), then doesn't that also imply that we are not perfect yet or we wouldn't need changing? So what is the Bible talking about? And how is it we are justified by faith alone if we apparently need to be holy, meaning "without sin"? If you are the tiniest bit like I was, these are very real and consuming questions that may be haunting and tormenting you, keeping you from entering into the rest of God. So let's find out together with the help of the Holy Spirit how to assemble the pieces of the puzzle in perfect harmony.

Let's pray and invite the Lord into our journey, acknowledging Him and confessing that we, on our own, can't deliver ourselves and that if we ever want to be free, He will have to do it.

Lord we ask You to help us. We ask You to draw us to You by Your Holy Spirit. We ask You to remove the religious veils from our eyes so that we can know You and know the truth. We ask You to open our understanding to the truth of your Word. We ask You to give us revelations that will set us free, because You said in Your Word that if we hold to Your teaching, we will know the truth and the truth will set us free (John 8:32). Deliver us completely from legalism, from every trace, shape, and form of it. Restore unto us the

Introduction

joy of our salvation and renew a right spirit within us that we may praise You again. In Jesus' name, amen.

* * *

For the Lord is our judge, the Lord is our law-giver, the Lord is our king; it is he who will save us.

—Isaiah 33:22 NIV

CHAPTER 1
MY DISCOVERY OF AND FALL FROM GRACE

In the short time I lived with both of my parents, Mama and Papa went through five separations. I was five years old, and my little brother, Clément, whom my mother called "Bébé," had just turned three.

"We're going to move into a big apartment far away" Mama told us one day.

"Yeah!" Brother and I expressed. "We won't see our downstairs neighbors anymore!" As far as Brother and I were concerned, these little terrors had caused us enough grief.

I was too young to understand that Papa's work as an exotic dancer would make it difficult for us to stay in Arvida, Québec, where everybody knows everyone. Mama wanted to avoid her two children being ridiculed as a result. So we packed up our little home and headed to Roxton Pond where we would trade the frequent, if somewhat volatile, presence of our father for two or three lengthy visits from him each year instead. Their tumultuous relationship finally ended in divorce.

On my first day of kindergarten, I boldly asked Mama if I could walk to school by myself.

"Are you sure, Sweetie? You don't want me to go with you?" Mama's love for her daughter was reaching out as always.

"Yes, Mama. I am sure. I can do it by myself! Please let me." Mama looked me over one more time and granted my request. "Okay, Sweetie, but *do not* cross the street, there is no need for that because the school is on the same side of the road."

15

Though Mama never told me at the time, she followed me at a distance for a week to make sure her dear daughter was safe and followed her rule.

When I first walked into my classroom, there was a boy playing with little cars or trucks. What fun! This would be my first friend. I hurried over to him. "May I play with you?"

"No!" he sharply replied.

I stepped back with sadness in my heart and quickly withdrew from him. For some reason, I didn't rise above that *no* but retreated inside myself. Would any of the kids ever want to play with me? Was something wrong with me? Was I different? Surely that meant I was unlovable, unacceptable.

During those early years and my later elementary years, I was introduced to the painful and damaging reality that rejection is. At some point, I started dance lessons, but ultimately dropped out. If I recall correctly, it is my feelings of inferiority that got the better of me. How could I dance in the midst of and in front of other kids while feeling so insecure and so inferior? The humiliation wasn't worth it. The teacher called home asking why I had stopped. She offered free classes if the reason was that we couldn't afford it; she said I had dancing in my blood and she didn't want to see that talent wasted because we couldn't pay. But I insisted I didn't want to go anymore, and Mama didn't force me.

We were poor, but Mama was always able to feed us. We didn't have the fancy clothes, but we had her love. We meant the world to her.

Back in Arvida, Mama found her place of belonging in a secret society that practiced the occult. She was able to get involved in the Granby chapter after we moved to Roxton Pond, and she got me and Brother involved in it too. One year, Mama was even asked to fulfill the function of master in our region, so in each ritual she would be the main officer. I became what they called "the dove," depicting purity, and I would walk specific steps waving incense and going from stand to stand to each particular officer. Mama was also involved with tarot cards and numerology. She read many books on metaphysics, believing it was spiritual. The ancient Egyptian culture attracted her, and she painted many occultist paintings and built pyramids and the like. At some point, she had a room in the house where all her occultist arts were. She began selling them at sales. In her mind, God was real and He was with her. Therefore, out of that belief, she took tarot cards seriously and spent many hours studying so she could tell her clients the truth. She was driven to get her readings right and was very much concerned about getting it wrong.

The summer I turned eleven, we moved to the Camping Tropicana in Granby and, a few years later, into the heart of Granby. This ended up being a real blessing in disguise. I was able to abandon the painful years of rejection and actually make friends. I ended up enjoying the remaining school years.

One day, when I was eleven or twelve years old, I was listening to some music, and I remembered what Mama told me the dance teacher had said, "She has dancing in her blood." The thing is, I had been visiting a friend of mine and we would dance in her bedroom for fun. However, I wasn't able to flow well, and I actually felt so stiff; it was like I just couldn't dance. So that day, standing in my bedroom and listening to some music, I said to God in faith, "You know, I remember my mom saying to me that the dance teacher had said I have it in my blood, but I just can't seem to be able to dance. I want to be able to dance like the teacher said." I wasn't a Christian at the time, but for some reason, awareness of God and childlike faith rose in me and I asked. And He gave freely without finding fault. At that moment, I felt the rhythm of the music flow through my body from the top of my head down to my feet, and when this happened I immediately knew how to dance. I knew how to move. From that day on, I absolutely loved dancing. It was something I could feel; it became such a part of me, as if I were one with the music.

Even though I had this early encounter with God, I increasingly professed to be an atheist. I had become sexually active around this same time (age thirteen, though I was introduced to some level of sexual activity by the time I was eleven) and was also attracted for a time to the mysterious dark side and the supernatural. I had started drawing pictures depicting darkness, evil, and the Devil himself in the form of a beast. The latter was the portrait of an open vision I had one day. I could see flames move and hear the sound of fire. I saw the face of a black beast. When I heard his breath as he opened his mouth to tell me something, I opened my eyes. I was so disappointed I didn't keep my eyes closed so I could hear what he had to tell me. Soon after, I had another vision where I saw three skeletons each wearing a robe and a hood on their head. I called them the three wise men of Satan.

At the time when I became sexually active, I was removed as "the dove" of our secret society. We were receiving monthly monographs which provided teaching and "spiritual experience." There were degrees to reach, and each of those monographs were intended to help reach those levels. Before my removal as "the dove," I was studying them faithfully.

However, I began to withdraw from reading them after my removal from that office. I eventually drifted away from this secret society, its practices, and its teachings altogether. Mama and Brother were still deep into the occult when I began to be more intellectually minded. Faith, God, the supernatural, they didn't make sense to me anymore. I despised people who professed a belief in God. What a waste of time to pray to someone who didn't exist. In my mind, a person would really have to be simple to believe in God.

In my early teens, I suffered from anorexia which was countered by light bulimia; I was tormented with my appearance, my weight, my calorie intake, and food. I also began to drink alcohol. My life revolved around my boyfriends and intensive workouts, besides school of course. I also had passing suicidal thoughts and was profoundly troubled about who I was. My identity was a black hole to me. By the time I reached my mid-twenties, I had probably had different sexual relationships in the double digits. One of them was a twenty-five-year-old man I dated when I was fifteen.

As I grew up, I became a very difficult daughter to my mother. The same was true of Brother. We did not respect her and we caused her great pain.

In Québec we have a middle school between high school and university, the CEGEP, which really serves as the bridge between the two. Depending on what you are aiming to specialize in, the program lasts for two to three years. Though my mathematics were average in high school, I began to excel in mathematics in CEGEP and decided to pursue a career as an actuary. I was accepted to Laval University in Québec City in Actuarial Sciences, which would take three years to complete.

While at the university, I loved partying. I also began drinking more and more. By the time I was in my last year, I was ordering cases of beer which were delivered to my door on campus. I was drinking beer every night even while studying for my final exams.

I met a guy, Steven, my first week at the university and we ultimately became engaged. Steven was also a student in Actuarial Sciences and he was one of the smart ones, the ones who assisted the teachers. He graduated one year earlier than I did and he ended up moving to Montreal for work.

I found a summer co-op job in an insurance company in Montreal between my second and third year at the university. I would use the subway to commute back and forth from my summer job. One day, while I was waiting on the platform for the train to arrive, a strange man began to harass and push me. I managed to make it onto the train car, but he followed me on. He continued to openly harass me until another man finally intervened and told him to stop. This encounter had me so shaken that as soon as I returned to the university for my last year of school, I enrolled in a self-defense ju-jitsu class being taught on campus.

I met a German guy, Kurt, during those classes. Alexander (the ju-jitsu teacher), Kurt, and I became very good friends. Kurt was extremely romantic and made me feel like I was a princess in a fairy tale. Before long we began seeing each other. The problem was, he had a girlfriend who lived in France and I was still engaged to Steven, who was now in Montreal. But that didn't stop either of us. By the time graduation arrived, I was faced with a choice. Jobs in Actuarial Sciences could only be found in the big cities. My options were Montreal, Québec City, or Toronto. If I went to Montreal, I would be reunited with Steven, and we could be married. But if I found a job in Québec City, I would probably end up with Kurt. I wanted to be able to decide for myself who I would live with, so Toronto looked like the best option. I would stay for a few months, learn English as a side bonus, make up my mind, and then move to either Montreal or Québec City based on my decision.

Although Toronto was my focus, I looked for openings in Montreal and Québec City as well, because I didn't want to end up with no job either. As a result, two companies contacted me, one from Montreal and one from Toronto, and I had my first interview with both.

Despite having some English classes in elementary school and high school, I couldn't really speak English at the time. At the university, some of the manuals were in English, which wasn't too much of an issue, because math and equations are all the same whether written in French or in English. Montreal was a bilingual city, but was still primarily French and was in a French province, so I wasn't too concerned about my lack of English skills. Most of the interview was in French, but they surprised me by asking two or three questions in English. I struggled to understand, and I wasn't really able to answer those questions.

Toronto was going to be even more of a challenge. It was an Anglophone city, and the interview was going to be conducted primarily in English. The first interview was done over the phone and the director of the actuarial department, Olivie, was a French Canadian too. What a relief that I could do the entire interview in French. At the end of the interview, though, she asked me a couple of questions in English and quickly realized I wasn't fluent. But she was pleased with the interview and as a result she contacted me for a second interview, in person, at the Toronto office, all in English! I accepted the challenge, and we scheduled the interview for a Friday.

I needed to strengthen my English fast if I wanted to have any chance of being able to do a whole interview in English, never mind getting the job. So I looked for someone I knew who could lodge me for a week in the area of Toronto prior to the interview in hopes of practicing just enough to at least be able to do the interview. I found an English-speaking acquaintance who lived in Waterloo that I had met during my summer co-op job. He agreed to house me the week of my interview, and I arrived at his place the weekend before. My plan to interact with him and his roommates didn't work, so I went to the convenience store at the end of the street, determined to find someone that was willing to speak English with me. I was able to find a couple of people who would speak with me and managed to get just enough practice to survive the interview.

The interview was led by Olivie and Richard, one of the department's managers who couldn't speak French. I did the whole interview in English, speaking slowly. I had to concentrate very hard to understand their questions and give them an appropriate answer. I would look at the ceiling as I searched for my words. At the end of the interview they decided to give me a break and allowed me to answer the last few questions in French. Richard had gotten enough information from me by now and Olivie completed the interview that way. They shared with me later that it was like someone else was sitting in front of them. I became lively and was speaking faster and with enthusiasm. This allowed them to see my personality, too. They ended up offering me the job.

22

Yes, that's right; the company in the French city turned me down because of my English, and the company in the English city hired me.

I never returned to Québec. Instead, Kurt broke up with his girlfriend and followed me to Toronto where we lived together for maybe a year and a half. Eventually a new employee, Brian, joined our department at work. He was a Christian, and his faith in God triggered a sincere question in me. How could an intelligent man like him believe in God? This question wasn't arrogant and it wasn't coming from a heart of ridicule. It was a genuine question for me. We began to chat here and there, and as a result he shared some of his experiences with God with me. I associated them with emotional reactions of sorts. I proudly went on to share with him my own supernatural experiences on the dark side. When he confessed that he believed in a real heaven and real hell, I thought this guy was a nut.

One morning, a group of colleagues were gathered together for a chat. Brian didn't glance my way the entire time. What was going on with him? When we all dispersed, I asked him if we could talk. He reluctantly agreed and eventually confessed that he had decided to avoid me because he was attracted to me. The Bible said he should not be unequally yoked with unbelievers, so he was going to keep his distance.

This man who was a Christian and wasn't supposed to be with someone like me was attracted to me? Well, I wasn't about to let that go. My heart was torn. Brian's heart was torn also, because he knew what the Scriptures said but he increasingly found me appealing. I shared with Kurt the situation, and having a very open mind, he told me I could meet with Brian, and he would give me time to make up my mind. Because of that, I felt released to hang out with Brian for a while. So at home I had Kurt, and at work I had Brian.

I was intrigued by the Christian music Brian was listening to in the car; it was good music. However, I wasn't too keen about the words. I longed for him to experience what the music of the world had to offer, and I was hoping for him to give it a try. On one occasion at his place, he prayed for me out loud. It was sweet. I had never heard such a thing. He eventually asked if I wanted to go to church. Because I was interested in him and in what concerned him, I accepted. I don't remember what the Pastor spoke about. After the sermon, Brian asked me if I wanted to go to the altar for prayer and I accepted. One of the youth pastors prayed over me. Nothing happened. I went back home.

I believe it was the next Thursday, I was at home studying for a professional exam. Kurt was at work that day. In Actuarial Sciences, not only do we have to earn a relevant degree at a university, but we also have to complete a number of professional exams to be a certified Actuary. Usually the company gave us paid study days. This was one of those days. I took a break and went to the piano and began to play. As the music from the piano filled the room, I thought, *I will give what Brian believes a chance and if, let's say, I see in six months or so that there is nothing to it, I will just come out of Christianity and stop going to church.* To my surprise, when I said these words to myself, I believed! Literally, I felt peace and joy flood my soul. The Holy Spirit had just taken residence in my heart. Alleluia!

Brian had told me that if I wanted to be saved I had to pray the sinner's prayer and he had left with me a booklet with the prayer in it. Like a little child, I grabbed the booklet and prayed the prayer to secure my salvation. I was already saved through believing and with the Holy Spirit coming into my heart, but I knew absolutely nothing about anything. So I did what Brian had told me and prayed the prayer. I didn't understand the prayer, especially the part about our sins being placed on the cross and being forgiven, but I prayed it. I was saved. I was twenty-five years old and I had finally started truly living. God's grace belonged to me.

It must have been maybe three days later that the Devil sought to steal from me what I had freely received that day. I was on the phone with Alexander, and I told him that I had just become a Christian.

"What? Kathleen, no! This is crazy. You've got to get out of that as fast as you can. Did you know that Christians don't even believe women have souls?"

"Alexander, be careful!" I interjected. "Don't say these things! My faith is still so young and fragile. Don't do that to me. You could cause me to lose it if you continue like this."

"That's exactly what needs to happen Kathleen. You need to drop this before it is too late."

I couldn't believe what I was hearing. I was devastated. And by the time we hung up, I was crying. This was a crossroad. *Do I return to my old life and give up this whole Christianity thing, or do I continue on my new journey with God?* Literally at that moment, God allowed me to supernaturally feel Him in my soul; I clearly recognized that if I gave up what I had just received, I was going to lose my entire universe. That day I decided to continue as a Christian even if it meant potentially losing my friend whom I dearly loved.

Now that I was a Christian, Brian and I could be together, and I knew I had to break up with Kurt and move out.

So I moved out and into the first apartment I could find. It was expensive but it would have to do, I was just happy I had found something so quickly.

Soon after that, the Lord instructed me to call Mama and apologize to her for all the pain I had caused in her life. God softened my heart, and I was able to slowly begin showing Mama true respect from this point on. The change in me was a great testimony to Mama of God's reality as I shared my newfound faith with her. I wanted her to know God for herself someday. She was, however, concerned for me.

"My daughter is in a sect!"

Mama had had two previous encounters with "Christians" in Roxton Pond. One Christian lady had provided food for our family when we were in need. But Mama was turned off because for religious reasons this lady wouldn't let her kids take off their long sleeves even though it was very hot that day. She would raise her voice and sternly warn them not to remove their long sleeves. Later, when we visited this lady's church, the women were not allowed to speak. None of them wore makeup, and they all had long hair and skirts or dresses.

The second experience she had was with a Christian lady who was always distraught after going to church or talking with her pastor. After church, she would tell Mama things like, "I have to make sure I don't talk too long on the phone or that I don't watch too much TV. The pastor said that when we do that we no longer have our focus on God. I need to focus on God!" and "The pastor said I'm paying too much attention to my dog, I need to keep my thoughts focused on God!" Mama could see that the church was not helping her friend to have any kind of peace.

And now her daughter had become one of these "Christians."

She was in inner turmoil toward my new attitude and behaviors. My language was different. Everything about me had changed. But she was confused by my insistence that Satan and hell were real and that the secret society and tarot cards she dealt in were not of God. Her curiosity (and the Holy Spirit) finally drew her to visit a local Pentecostal church where she truly encountered God's presence. It didn't take long before she came out a new creation. Alleluia!

Brian and I continued dating. I absolutely loved and trusted him with everything that was in me. But he became moody. He would get upset easily and would lose his temper with me. I had no idea what he was going through. A few months went by and out of nowhere he received four different job offers with amazing salaries which he couldn't refuse. He ended up leaving the company. Not long after, he was at my place and commented about my appearance in a way that was hurtful. I wanted to hide. He obviously wasn't happy with what he was seeing, so I calmly told him he had to leave. The next day, we talked over the phone and concluded that we needed to break up. What had happened with us? I was completely heartbroken. There was nothing left for me. Brian was my everything. At least I didn't have to face him daily at work. But I still had to see his name on different paperwork. A month later, I called him in tears, asking him if we could get back together. He was rather cold and he was firm. No was his answer.

During this time, my relationship with God grew stronger. I had been experiencing a lack of motivation for my exams and career in general as my heart was becoming more and more absorbed with God and the things of God. One day, sitting down in my apartment, studying for my sixth professional exam, I was listening to some secular music and was seriously debating whether to stop taking exams and focus on God and whatever His call was on my life. The song on the CD was playing Revelation 3:20 KJV: "Behold, I stand at the door, and knock: if any man hear my voice, and open the door, I will come in to him, and will sup with him, and he with me." I had never heard that Scripture in that song before, and I had heard that music many times!

That did it. I stopped taking exams from that day on and never looked back. I have always had peace about my decision, and I have never regretted it. I continued working in the field but with the understanding that this choice was going to limit my career. That day I chose to follow all that God had for me over my career.

About two months after my breakup with Brian, I was getting ready to go to work, tears streaming down my face. I was standing in front of the mirror in the washroom and I was trying to put my mascara on. Talk about a challenge, putting your mascara on while crying. I cried out to God, "You have to do something. I can't go on like this anymore." I finally composed myself, put my mascara on, and left for work.

During those days, I didn't have a car so my commute consisted of a ride on the bus followed by a ride on the subway. When sitting down in the subway, minding my own business, I had a vision. There in front of my eyes was me. I was sitting down on a one-person bench on the altar of a church (which was not the church I was attending at the time), and I was either teaching or preaching (I didn't hear what I was saying). I was facing the people sitting on pews on

My Discovery of and Fall From Grace

the right side of the church. This lasted for a while. Then I saw myself standing up, in the middle of the altar, singing. This lasted for a while. Then I began thinking while the vision was unfolding. The message God had given me was a testimony, specific to my experiences. I didn't have a wide biblical knowledge base to draw from, so I couldn't sustain preaching to only one church. Surely I would travel to many churches, telling about my testimonies. Ministry could also eventually open a door to feed hungry children.

Wow! I had just received a vision from God. Supernatural, amazing! But first and foremost, God had given me something to look forward to. He gave me a future. He gave me a purpose in life. When I felt that I had no future anymore without Brian, I now had a purpose; I had a call over my life. I became very much on fire for God from that day forward. Everybody at work knew I was a Christian. After work, I would put worship music on and worship for an hour or so almost every night in my little bachelor apartment. God began to speak to me in different ways. I also began to receive prophetic dreams about me, about others, and about nations. As I received them and acted upon them, God gave me more and more. The Word says that to him who has, more will be given.[1] Because I believed God and directed my life according to what He would show me in dreams, He saw that I was faithful with what He gave me, and He gave me more. I came to understand that not all dreams were direct interventions from God, but that one of the ways God speaks to His children is through dreams. And I began to expect God to speak to me when I went to bed at night. When I didn't know the meaning

---

[1] See Matthew 13:12.

29

of a dream God gave me, I would normally find the answer in the Word. The Holy Spirit would reveal to me what the symbols in my dream meant and the interpretation would always align with God's Word.

About three weeks after God gave me the vision on the subway, as had been my custom I spent time in worship after work. It was a Wednesday. While in worship, I thought, *I am a Christian now, so I can't go to bars anymore.* This realization came out of a heart of love for God. But bars were the only places I knew of where I could dance. This meant I was never going to dance again. That night, for the Lord, I gave up dancing.

Oh, but God is so good, I tell you! That Saturday I went to church to see a special minister, Steven Hill, who was visiting from the United States. When the service was over, I went to the altar. God had called me into the ministry about three weeks before and I wanted to know all the details about it. There was no altar call, I just went alone, just me and God, and I prayed and asked Him to reveal to me every detail of the call of God upon my life. Once I was done, I began to walk toward the exit of the sanctuary. There was a man whom I had never met and whom I have never seen since. He stood close to the exit in the aisle. As I got closer, he asked if he could speak to me and began to prophesy over my life. He gave me all of the details concerning the call of God upon my life. Not only was what he was telling me in line with the vision I had just received a few weeks back, but he gave me additional details. And one thing he said that really blessed my heart was, "God is showing me that you love to dance."

"Yes! I do!"

"He is showing me that you love to dance. God is grieving because His children don't dance. You will dance for eternity as the Father sings over you."

Brian was still in my thoughts and even though both the vision and prophesy gave me hope, joy, and a purpose, I was still hoping for Brian to come back. God began to show me that I needed to let him go, but I wasn't convinced yet. I was fortunate that Brian had also been a consistent attendant of another church in Kitchener, Ontario. This allowed him to go to that church instead of coming to the church I was now attending, Queensway Cathedral, in Etobicoke (which is now Church on the Queensway).

During those days, I spent time with a woman who attended my church, Advika. She loved the Lord, and she took upon herself to mentor me as a young believer. I began to go to the Friday night prayer meetings with her. I would take the subway to the closest station, and Advika would pick me up and drive me to church. However, this one Friday night was anything but ordinary. On our way to church, Advika and I talked about Brian. I don't remember why we started talking about Brian. Maybe I shared with her how I was holding onto hope that we would reunite.

"Kathleen, God showed Brian that you aren't the one for him."

"What?" I exclaimed. "What do you mean? How would you know that?"

"He told me. Before you broke up, God showed him that you were not the one."

No wonder Brian had been moody, losing his temper and acting strange. God had been telling him to end our relationship. Why hadn't he said anything to me? Why would he tell Advika?

I was one of the very few young adults to attend the prayer meetings. The group was small compared to the size of our church's congregation. Advika and I entered the sanctuary. Unlike our custom, she walked right to the second row and sat beside Paul.

Oh no . . . . Paul was six foot four and a half inches tall and sort of an odd character. He was letting his beard and hair grow as he was preparing to play Jesus in the Passion Play at our church. I didn't want to sit near anybody, let alone Paul. *What if he could hear me praying?* I took the seat next to Advika, with Paul on the other side of her.

Now that I knew for sure God's will wasn't for Brian and me to be together, I desired to be set free from Brian that very night. I didn't want to feel for him the way I did anymore. I wanted freedom. I wanted God to remove Brian from my future, because I now knew he didn't belong there anymore. The prayer meeting had not really started yet. However, I began to feel the Holy Spirit telling me to stand up. *I don't want to stand up. Everybody is sitting down!* But the Holy Spirit kept insisting and I kept pushing back. After a few back and forths, I finally stood up and began praying out loud, "Freedom! Freedom! Freedom! Tonight!" Suddenly the power of God touched my body; it was like electricity and tingling. It went through both my arms starting from my hands, and it also went through both my legs starting from my feet. Then I felt someone touching my forehead, but as far as I know, no one touched me. We began singing, and my voice was coming out with an unusual ease. *What was going on?*

Once the prayer meeting was over, Paul approached me and gave me some prophetic information about me—information the prophet had also revealed to me. I proceeded to essentially tell him how God had called me into the ministry.

"We will do it together, Kathleen. You and me."

Well, that meant I would never get married, because no man would allow me to do ministry with another man. But when Paul began talking about children it hit me. *Whoa! What? Paul? The tall weirdo of the church? Married to me?* God was in the house that night and the timing coincided so well with my request to be freed from Brian. I softened my heart to what Paul was saying. I sensed it was of God, but I obviously would need confirmation. However, I had a strong impression, I had a witness, that this was indeed God's will.

It had been about seven months since Brian and I broke up and we had just contacted each other that week and made plans to meet as friends the following Monday. Monday came and we went to a restaurant and afterward went to the youth service in my church. We got there, and to my surprise, Paul was there. Paul saw me and asked if he could sit with me and I said yes. Paul was on my left and Brian was on my right and I had both hands up. *God! Help me!*

On Wednesday, Brian called me very troubled.

"I've been so upset since I saw you," he said. "Had I known the pain you endured because of our breaking up, I would have come back to you. I want to get back with you."

Whoa! Talk about a divinely orchestrated test! "Didn't God show you that I wasn't the one for you?"

"Yes. But I also know that we have been given the right to exercise our free will."

"Well, what did God say to you, and how did He say it?"

Brian confessed he had been seeking God concerning whether I was the woman he should marry. One night the Lord gave him a dream. In the dream, names were drawn. A name was drawn and it was my name. Then a voice in the dream said, "No."

That night, I was placed in front of another crossroad: would I choose the man I had been longing for with everything that was in me, or would I choose God's will for my life? Was I willing to give up for God what I wanted the most and get married to a guy I didn't know and wasn't particularly fond of at the time?

Paul and I were married nine months later on August 9, 2003, and I am so glad that God was my matchmaker. I became pregnant a few months later and gave birth to Aaron on September 10, 2004.

About three years after we were married, we were led to Ebenezer Revival Tabernacle, a Pentecostal church operating under the Independent Assemblies of God International (Canada) (IAOGIC), located in Scarborough, Ontario. Relatively soon after we started attending that church, the Lord spoke to me in a dream with a prophecy that I would sing in the church. And He said, "It is time for you to take singing lessons." This was about seven years after the vision in the subway where I'd seen myself singing in the middle of the altar.

By faith, I began lessons. Learning how to sing was not easy for me. I had a hard time projecting my voice; it was like I had no voice for the longest time. A year and a half passed and hardly anyone at church knew that I took singing lessons.

Our senior pastor approached me one Sunday morning and asked if I wanted to be part of the worship team. He didn't even know if I could sing! I said yes by faith. I started singing on the team and they thought my mic wasn't working, because they couldn't hear my voice. It took me close to three years of singing lessons to finally experience a breakthrough and be able to project my voice. Oh, how I felt like giving up many times, but I thank God that I did not.

I became pregnant with our second son, Jonathan, and gave birth to him on December 22, 2007. We were out of the hospital just in time to celebrate Christmas with our three-day-old baby.

In January 2010, Paul and I became licensed ministers with the IAOGIC. God had confirmed His calling on our lives by fulfilling the ministry vision He'd given to us. Now that I was a minister, I carried a greater weight of responsibility and I needed more than ever to be an example of following Christ in obedience. God was first in my life, and I desired to be holy as He is holy.

While I looked successful on the outside, I began to spiral downward on the inside. Something wasn't right. I wasn't measuring up. I wasn't a good enough Christian. I began to lose my joy as I focused on my sins and the need to be better, to do better.

During this time, my family doctor feared I had a fairly common but serious chronic illness. This diagnosis triggered extreme fear in me. Where was my faith? It later proved to be a wrong diagnostic, but it exposed that something was terribly wrong in my heart. I also began having anxiety spells. Bursts of heat would flow through my body, and I would fear the worst. Other sicknesses were always in the realm of possibility, and I entertained all sorts of ideas about diseases in my body. I would literally cry in the doctor's office. I didn't want to die. I didn't want to suffer. I felt so terrible at how poor of a witness I was to the doctors. As a Christian, wasn't I supposed to be at peace even in the face of death? When I had given my heart to Jesus, there had been such peace and joy. How had I gotten to this place? What was wrong with me? This was the cry of my heart. And God, in His faithfulness, answered me.

CHAPTER 2
THE DEADLY POISON OF LEGALISM

Every day my thoughts raced out of control. *Isn't God obligated to reject me until I behave perfectly all the time? I really have to make sure I am not jealous toward anyone. I hope I am not. I really can't be proud when God uses me to minister to others. What will happen if I die the moment I experience jealousy or pride? What about if I lose my temper and then die? Oh, how I long to be loved unconditionally. Oh, how I long to be accepted just the way that I am. I can just see Him, disappointed in me, upset with me. I know He loves me, but He also commanded me to be holy. How can I be holy? I fall short so much. Am I going to hell? God, You are not the author of confusion. But I never know for sure if I am good enough or if I have done enough. I have to work harder, just to be safe, before it is too late. Oh, how I long for God to be pleased with me. Please, be pleased with me; I so want to do what's right.*

I could barely remember the time when my heart wasn't racing from the driving force to do better, be better, and from my endless quest to make sense of the grace of God. I was in a catastrophic situation. I was miserable. And I was under a sense of condemnation almost continually. My spiritual performance, my sins, and the need to witness with excellence tormented me. I was a Christian, but I definitely had no joy. And I could hardly sleep at night.

One day, driving home from work, I cried out to God in desperation. "God! What is wrong with me?" And that night, by the grace of God, I was able to fall asleep. God gave me two dreams in response to my cry.

In the first dream, God showed me that witchcraft was the problem in my life. *Witchcraft?* But I'd left the occult years ago, long before I even gave my life to Jesus. I'd also re-

37

nounced it and prayed a prayer of deliverance after I was saved. The dream seemed to indicate that if we were not exercising spiritual discernment, this sort of witchcraft could easily appear harmless to us. The Lord also revealed to me that the witchcraft had started small but grew until it infected my entire life. The Lord does warn us in His Word not to give the Devil a foothold.[1] I must have unknowingly done just that. He also showed me that I was now amongst the ones that the Bible warned against, saying "from such turn away."[2] Another very significant piece of information the Lord showed me that night was that I was working hard, but that my laboring was in vain because it was bearing no real fruit; it was not working out a change in me, and I was not being transformed from glory to glory as a result of that hard work. I was, in essence, doing what the Bible described as works of the flesh.

In the second dream, He exposed the hypocrisy of my life and my putting on of a façade to try to appear righteous before men. And the last thing He revealed to me, but also the most disturbing one, was the Father weeping because His daughter was gone.

To my terror, what I feared the most had come upon me; I was now a prodigal daughter, disconnected from my heavenly Father. My extreme attempt at keeping myself in right standing with God was the very thing that had led me away from Him. The thing I was desperately trying to avoid by working so hard to live the Christian life was the very thing that had caused my worse fear to come to pass.

The severity of my situation was so great that I had come to a place where I was feeling disconnected not only

---

[1] See Ephesians 4:27.
[2] 2 Timothy 3:5 KJV.

from God but also from my husband, Paul, and my kids, Aaron and Jonathan. Though I was with them physically and though I longed for them, my spirit felt disconnected from them.

God had not moved from me; His heart had not changed toward me. But through believing lies and submitting to another,[3] I had moved from Him. I am the one who withdrew myself from the Lord, from the one who loved me the most. I had changed, and all He wanted was for me to come home. I am so grateful that God heard my cry of distress that day and responded that very night! And He will hear yours, too, as you cry to Him with your whole heart.

I knew that morning that somehow the answer to my question of the day before resided in understanding the witchcraft part. "Witchcraft?" I asked God. "How can this be? I don't understand. I mean, I am not involved in any occult practices, nothing. How can witchcraft be my problem?"

I went into our home office that morning and sat down beside the desk, absorbed with the dreams I had just received. There happened to be a book written by Derek Prince entitled *Lucifer Exposed: The Devil's Plans to Destroy Your Life* sitting on our office desk. Still wondering about the witchcraft part of the first dream, I casually picked up the book and randomly opened it. The sentence my eyes fell on was this: "Wherever we encounter legalism, somewhere behind it is witchcraft."[4] My eyes widened. *Oh my goodness!* You can be sure that God had all my attention then. As I began reading that section of

---

[3] That is, submitting to the law unknowingly.
[4] Derek Prince, *Lucifer Exposed: The Devil's Plans to Destroy Your Life* (New Kensington, Penn.: Whitaker House, 2006), 83.

the book, to my amazement I quickly realized that legalism described exactly what I was going through.

What is legalism? Simply put, legalism is trying to walk the Christian walk in our own strength, in our own ability, by our own self-effort. It is relying on self instead of relying on the Holy Spirit. It is submitting to rules and regulations, to a law (thus the word *legal*(lawful)•*ism*), instead of submitting to Christ. It is placing principles before people.[5] It is trying to live by the letter without knowing the Spirit (the One who wrote it) or the spirit (the real intent and purpose) behind it.

The Power Behind Legalism

> O you poor and silly and thoughtless and unreflecting and senseless Galatians! Who has fascinated or *bewitched* or cast a spell over you, unto whom—right before your very eyes—Jesus Christ (the Messiah) was openly and graphically set forth and portrayed as crucified?
>
> —Galatians 3:1 (emphasis added)

We see in Galatians 3:1 that the apostle Paul used the word *bewitched* to describe the state of the Galatians. Derek Prince pointed out in *Lucifer Exposed* that wherever we encounter legalism, somewhere behind it is witchcraft.[6] As I studied his book along with the Scriptures and my own experience, I learned that the supreme aim of witchcraft in the church is to hide the reality of the work of the cross, Jesus

---

[5] See Matthew 12:1-8; Mark 2:27.
[6] Prince, *Lucifer Exposed*, 83.

Christ crucified.[7] We also know from the Word of God that rebellion is as the sin of witchcraft.[8] "The illegitimate power that supports rebellion is the power of witchcraft."[9] I began to understand what Derek Prince meant when he highlighted that what makes witchcraft so dangerous is the fact that it is within the church and is working against the people who are unaware of its presence[10]; God had showed me that this sort of witchcraft can easily be dismissed as innocent and inoffensive. Thus, witchcraft was the main problem in the Galatian church; they had returned to fleshly endeavors to please God; "they had reverted to keeping all sorts of rules as a way of achieving righteousness with God."[11] Witchcraft is not only an evil supernatural power, but it is also a work of the flesh.[12]

I believe it was a year before God showed me that legalism was my problem, but I can't be certain on the timing. Paul had decided to fast for me three days due to the seriousness of my situation. At the end of the three days, God revealed to him three things. One of them came through a dream. In the dream, we were in church. I was sitting down in a pew in the row in front of him, which allowed him to see better what was happening to me. There were some suspicious church people who were administering a questionable medicine to me, and I was visibly in a daze as though under a spell. Even at that time God had been revealing the evil power of witchcraft that was at work in my life. But during the time I was under the spell of legalism, I was not able to grasp the

---

[7] See Prince, *Lucifer Exposed*, 80, 113–114.
[8] See 1 Samuel 15:23. To be discussed in more detail in Chapter 3.
[9] Prince, *Lucifer Exposed*, 91.
[10] Prince, *Lucifer Exposed*, 79, 98.
[11] Prince, *Lucifer Exposed*, 81.
[12] See Galatians 5:20.

revelation of what it really meant to us that Christ was cruci-fied to pay the price for our sins. I was constantly studying the Word, but I had a hard time coming to the true knowledge of it.[13] I was desperately searching to know the truth; the ex-treme torment of it became unbearable. Legalism is a cruel master.

Although legalism being a form of witchcraft was a new idea to me, years before I fell deep into legalism the Lord had spoken to me very clearly about the satanic powers that are behind witchcraft. It was during the time my mother was involved in the occult and was a tarot cards apprentice. In a dream, the Lord had showed me my mom's dog. The dog was crazy, running aimlessly across the street. He looked like he was in a daze; he looked like a zombie. His eyes wide open, he was running without clear direction—on the street, off the street, on the street, off the street. As I watched this disturbing scene, the Lord spoke to me and said, "They torment you and they give you no rest."

Now that I understand legalism as a form of witchcraft, this dream from years ago holds even more meaning for me. Certainly after having suffered under the hard taskmaster that legalism is, I can testify that the spirits of witchcraft torment you and they give you no rest for your soul. As far as what we are talking about in this book, you become obsessed with your spiritual performance and with your need to meet God's expectations. You find yourself constantly under a death sen-tence because every day your failures make you worthy of hell. You keep thinking about how you need to change, how

---

[13] See 2 Timothy 3:7.

The Deadly Poison of Legalism

you don't measure up; and it seems like the more you try, the worse you become.

In Galatians 5:20, witchcraft is listed as a work of the flesh. In the flesh, what you are trying to avoid is exactly what you end up doing, and what you are trying to do is exactly what you never seem to be able to do. Now, doesn't that sound familiar? In the following Scripture, the apostle Paul describes a similar situation that he found himself in:

> For I do not understand my own actions [I am baffled, bewildered]. I do not practice or accomplish what I wish, but I do the very thing that I loathe [which my moral instinct condemns]. Now if I do [habitually] what is contrary to my desire, [that means that] I acknowledge and agree that the Law is good (morally excellent) and that I take sides with it. However, it is no longer I who do the deed, but the sin [principle] which is at home in me and has possession of me. For I know that nothing good dwells within me, that is, in my flesh. I can will what is right, but I cannot perform it. [I have the intention and urge to do what is right, but no power to carry it out.] For I fail to practice the good deeds I desire to do, but the evil deeds that I do not desire to do are what I am [ever] doing. Now if I do what I do not desire to do, it is no longer I doing it [it is not myself that acts], but the sin [principle] which dwells within me [fixed and operating in my soul]. So I find it to be a law (rule of action of my being) that when I want to do what is right

43

and good, evil is ever present with me and I am subject to its insistent demands. For I endorse and delight in the Law of God in my inmost self [with my new nature]. But I discern in my bodily members [in the sensitive appetites and wills of the flesh] a different law (rule of action) at war against the law of my mind (my reason) and making me a prisoner to the law of sin that dwells in my bodily organs [in the sensitive appetites and wills of the flesh]. O unhappy and pitiable and wretched man that I am! Who will release and deliver me from [the shackles of] this body of death? O thank God! [He will!] through Jesus Christ (the Anointed One) our Lord! So then indeed I, of myself with the mind and heart, serve the Law of God, but with the flesh the law of sin.[14]

This sounds like someone who is tormented to me! So we see that when the apostle Paul was trying to obey the law in his own strength it only brought him misery. I really like another statement that Derek Prince said in his book: "Christianity is not a religion of doing our best or a religion of effort. But rather it is a union with Christ, it is a relationship. If we truly unite with the Holy Spirit within us we will bring forth the fruit of the Spirit. If we unite with the flesh, no matter how many rules we set in order to keep the flesh in order, we will bring forth the fruit of the flesh."[15]

---

[14] Romans 7:15–25.
[15] Prince, *Lucifer Exposed*, 130.

We must shun the works of the flesh. Trying to save ourselves, trying to change ourselves, and trying to keep ourselves in our own strength are all works of the flesh. As we learn more about the finished work of Jesus on the cross, we will find ourselves able to rest in His work. Knowledge of Him and His work combined with the understanding that the flesh profits us nothing[16] set us free to leave the works of the flesh behind.

Spiritual Adultery

Do you not know, brethren—for I am speaking to men who are acquainted with the Law—that legal claims have power over a person only for as long as he is alive? For [instance] a married woman is bound by law to her husband as long as he lives; but if her husband dies, she is loosed and discharged from the law concerning her husband. Accordingly, she will be held an adulteress if she unites herself to another man while her husband lives. But if her husband dies, the marriage law no longer is binding on her [she is free from that law]; and if she unites herself to another man, she is not an adulteress. Likewise, my brethren, you have undergone death as to the Law through the [crucified] body of Christ, so that now you may belong to Another, to Him Who was raised from the dead in order that we may bear fruit for God. When we were living in

---

[16] See John 6:63.

the flesh (mere physical lives), the sinful passions that were awakened and aroused up by [what] the Law [makes sin] were constantly operating in our natural powers (in our bodily organs, in the sensitive appetites and wills of the flesh), so that we bore fruit for death. But now we are discharged from the Law and have terminated all intercourse with it, having died to what once restrained and held us captive. So now we serve not under [obedience to] the old code of written regulations, but [under obedience to the promptings] of the Spirit in newness [of life].

—Romans 7:1–6

During my struggle with legalism, I had recurring dreams where I was back with my old boyfriends again and dreams where I had sexual affairs with other men even though, in reality, I was married to Paul. I was disturbed by these dreams, especially because in real life I had no desire for any of this! I somehow sensed that these dreams were either from God or at least were allowed by God and that they carried a meaning. But at the time, I could not understand their meaning. It was clear that God was not telling me to return to my old lovers, for this would have been completely unscriptural. I sought God regarding the dreams regularly. When God began to show me that legalism was spiritual adultery, I finally understood the meaning of these persistent dreams. Legalism, just like Romans 7:1-6 plainly demonstrate, is spiritual adultery; it is going back to an old lover, the law. The Bible says that Christ, our bridegroom, our heavenly husband, came to set us free from the law.[17] We have died to the law so that we may belong to Christ.

We can know what we treasure the most by what's on our mind the most. Jesus says it this way in Luke 12:34: "For where your treasure is, there will your heart be also." What's on our mind most of the time is the object of our attention and of our affection. How would you like it if your spouse constantly thought about someone else? Or do you remember when you first met your spouse? They probably were on your mind most of the time, weren't they? Well, it's the same thing with God. He wants to be on our mind. He wants to be what we want, what we desire, and what we love the most; He wants to be the object of our attention and of our affection. The Bible is full of Scriptures that demonstrate we are on His mind, we are what He wants, we are what He desires. He wants our heart and it hurts His heart and displeases Him when our affection begins to shift to someone or to something else and when we start to enjoy or to trust in someone or something else instead of Him. That is why, as the bride of Christ, when we place our trust in ourselves or in the law to make us righteous, we become adulterous because we do so while married to Christ. Does not the Bible say that we must guard our heart with all diligence for out of it flows the issues of life?[18]

If our trust is entirely in Christ, our mind will habitually remain on Him, the object of our trust. The prophet Isaiah says it this way in Isaiah 26:3: "You will guard him and keep him in perfect and constant peace whose mind [both its inclination and its character] is stayed on You, because he com-

---

[17] See Galatians 5:1.
[18] See Proverbs 4:23 KJV.

mits himself to You, leans on You, and hopes confidently in You." However, if our trust is in ourselves and our own ability to obey the law, our mind will be centered on ourselves, on our performance, or the lack thereof, as well as on the law which we must somehow meet. But the Bible tells us in Exodus 34:14 that God is a jealous God and He will not tolerate to share us with another. He wants exclusivity of heart. Just like we demand exclusivity of heart from our spouse, God is looking for the same from us. We are married to God,[19] and there is no difference between being married to God and being married to our spouse in the sense that both will expect from us total faithfulness. Now that being said, God is good and He knows our weaknesses! He is more than willing to take us just as we are unto the way we are going even if we are struggling with spiritual adultery while we have a repentant heart. Where God has a problem is when we continue to tolerate sin without the desire and willingness to turn away from it, for as a healthy child of God, when we have a genuine will to turn from it, our natural response will be to seek God for help to enable us to overcome it. And we know from the Word that God is quick to forgive and abundant in grace and mercy. "O taste and see that the Lord is good: blessed is the man that trusteth in him."[20]

Most of us would never think of backsliding in sin and yet have backslidden into something that makes sin's power even stronger in our lives: spiritual adultery[21]. Attempting to reach right standing with God by complying and submitting to rules and regulations instead of obeying Christ by placing

---

[19] See Isaiah 54:5; Revelation 22:17.
[20] Psalm 34:8 KJV.
[21] See 1 Corinthians 15:56.

our trust in Him and in Him crucified is spiritual adultery. We can either trust Christ and His finished work at the cross, or we can trust the law to make us right; but we can't trust both at the same time. Galatians 5:18 reveals to us that we have only two options: dependence upon the Holy Spirit or dependence upon the law. "But if ye be led of the Spirit, ye are not under the law."[22] We are either under the law (any law) or under grace, but we cannot be under both.

> For I am zealous for you with a godly eagerness and a divine jealousy, for I have betrothed you to one Husband, to present you as a chaste virgin to Christ. But [now] I am fearful, lest that even as the serpent beguiled Eve by his cunning, so your minds may be corrupted and seduced from wholehearted and sincere and pure devotion to Christ. For [you seem readily to endure it] if a man comes and preaches another Jesus than the One we preached, or if you receive a different spirit from the [Spirit] you [once] received or a different gospel from the one you [then] received and welcomed; you tolerate [all that] well enough!
>
> —2 Corinthians 11:2–4

Another Gospel

I am surprised and astonished that you are so quickly turning renegade and deserting Him Who invited and called you by the grace (un-

---

[22] Galatians 5:18.

merited favor) of Christ (the Messiah) [and that you are transferring your allegiance] to a different [even an opposition] gospel. Not that there is [or could be] any other [genuine Gospel], but there are [obviously] some who are troubling and disturbing and bewildering you [with a different kind of teaching which they offer as a gospel] and want to pervert and distort the Gospel of Christ (the Messiah) [into something which it absolutely is not].

—Galatians 1:6–7

One student asked me during Sunday school one Easter Sunday, "What difference is there between how it was before Jesus came and after He came? Nothing seems to be much different between before His coming on earth and after. Things seem to be the same now as before He came."

What a good question that was! O but that we may understand the difference! The difference is night and day; and if we do not understand the difference that Jesus really makes in our lives, we will be at risk for the Enemy to use our lack of knowledge to deceive us and ensnare us. In what way can the Enemy entrap us? He can lure us into legalism.

Remember, legalism is trying to walk the Christian walk in our own strength. It is trying to save and to keep ourselves by our own efforts, self-righteousness, spiritual works, spiritual performance, and accomplishments. One may even believe that he is saved by grace through faith alone, but yet may try to reach perfection in his own human effort, wisdom, and willpower. Such a one needs to ask himself, what then does Christ add to this equation? And even if one believes that salvation is by faith alone, what does Christ have to do with his sanctification and with the keeping of his soul? And that is the problem—Christ and Christ crucified is sadly no longer part of the equation for the legalist. Legalism will subtly, slowly, and over a period of time, enter into one's life unnoticed. Its goal is to remove Christ and Christ crucified from the equation so that one day you wake up and you are back at trying to save your own soul again in your own strength. One may even start as very devoted to the Lord, but, due to lack of revelation knowledge in this area, may be lured away into the different gospel of legalism through the crafty deception of the Enemy. Galatians 3:3 puts it this way: "Are you so foolish and so senseless and so silly? Having begun [your new life spiritually] with the [Holy] Spirit, are you now reaching perfection [by dependence] on the flesh?"

Legalism is another gospel, not that there is any other genuine gospel. It is trying to live the Christian life void of the Spirit of God. It is of utmost importance for us to understand that God hasn't called us to try, but to believe. I like the way Beth Moore puts it in her book *Breaking Free*. When exploring the place where performance has replaced passion, she says: "If our motivation for obedience is anything other than love for and devotion to God, we're probably up to our eyeballs in legalism and in for disaster. Obedience without love is nothing but the law."[23] You may have started in the Spirit but have ended up dry and fearful with a lot of laws and regulations you need to comply with if you want to have any chance of making it. What will happen if you don't have time to confess the impure thought that just crossed your mind before you

---

[23] Beth Moore, *Breaking Free: Making Liberty in Christ a Reality in Life* (Nashville: B&H Publishing Group, 2000), 77–78.

die? One minute you may be at risk of going to hell; the next minute you may be okay for heaven. It is a very unstable and frightening place in which you live day after day. What you are left with is a relationship with the law (any law) instead of sweet fellowship with the Lord. Love no longer reigns in your heart, but rather a dreadful feeling that if you do not measure up, you won't make it in. Not only that, but it is also a place where you are all too aware that you don't measure up or that you can't measure up. It is a state where you no longer *receive and enjoy* the love of God. Instead, you live in constant fear that God is displeased with you and that He is disappointed in you. You are haunted by the fear of failure.

Brothers and sisters, there has got to be a better way. If the gospel of Christ is indeed the good news, then surely this can't be what Christ died to give us. There has got to be something, somewhere, that is not adding up in this equation. It is important to not just stay there but to seek God's counsel by prayer and by studying the Word until clarity and deliverance come. And ah! Doesn't the Bible say that we must labor to enter into the rest of God?[24] This is where laboring becomes appropriate, and I did need to labor to enter into the rest of God. Not a labor in the flesh, but a labor that consisted of many tears before the Lord, prayer, waiting on God, and studying the Word.

Paul and I witnessed an incident early in our marriage. It was a Friday night, and during those days, I took Fridays off from work, not paid, to spend that time with God. Well, I have to admit that my spirit was willing but my flesh was weak, because I didn't accomplish much during those Fri-

---

[24] See Hebrews 4:11 KJV.

days. It seems like I was always distracted with something else. Still, I wanted to do more for the Lord, and I was willing to try taking one day off a week for that very purpose. Anyway, that night, Paul and I drove to the convenience store to get a few items, never expecting anything like what we were about to witness.

Lo and behold, when we got to the counter to pay for our items, there were three people in front of us: one woman and two men. The woman was speaking in tongues while putting her items on the counter, right there in front of the cashier. She had a serious look on her face, and she didn't even address the cashier. She was just seriously praying in tongues while the other two men were just standing by her side. The cashier rang up her total as though nothing unusual was going on. I was stunned! It was as if she were living in another world, disconnected from this world altogether and hardly interacting with it.

Since the woman had been praying, we assumed the three considered themselves to be Christians and went to talk with them outside of the convenience store. The woman went straight to the car and sat in the back seat as if she were too good to mingle with us. The two men (who we discovered were her followers) talked with us, seeking to fulfill their mission. One was with my husband and one was with me. Each group was a few feet apart so we couldn't hear what the others were discussing.

The man who talked with me showed me a newspaper page with a young lady wearing jeans and told me of the "great calling" that God had placed on his leader's life. His "prophetess" had been "called" by God to warn women not to wear pants, not to wear makeup, and not to dye their hair.

They were to dress modestly and without extravagance. He was very strict about it, telling me that we had to stick to what the Scriptures said. He then opened his Bible and showed me some Scriptures that anyone without any proper understanding of the context or the whole counsel of the Word of God could interpret the way he did.

Now, in those days, I was hardly wearing skirts and dresses, I much preferred pants. I was amazed, however, at the timing, because that night, I happened to wear a skirt! He looked at me from top to bottom and said something like, "That's good; that's good. You are wearing a skirt, you do not wear makeup, and you are dressed modestly." Oh dear! I *was* wearing makeup; it was just natural in color. I was wearing a skirt, yes, but that wasn't a true representation of what I would normally wear. And I had dyed my hair blond; it just looked very natural on me. I told him I was, in fact, dying my hair blond, to which he responded something like, "Well, I guess there is a woman at our church who dyes her hair, and she is anointed too." He needed to make up his mind. Was God for or against such practices? God wouldn't anoint her like that if He wasn't okay with her "sinful" hair dyeing.

Paul and I were appalled at what we witnessed that night. The woman isolated herself from us. For someone who was such a "great woman of God," there was no love radiating from her. She didn't reach out to us. She didn't reach out to *me*, a young woman to whom she was supposedly called to save and minister. She had no desire to fellowship with us or to pour on us the love of God or, if anything, to share any wisdom or revelation that she had apparently received from God. I felt very saddened. These men were so deceived that they were no longer following God but rather following a deluded, self-centered, and self-exalting woman, and they did not even know it. They were following a useless, empty doctrine that brought no life, but only condemnation. They were following something that had no ability to rescue the people who were going to hell—the people who were distressed, emotionally wounded and bruised, abused, and discouraged.

Was that the gospel Christ had in mind when He bled and died on the cross? Was that what drove Him to suffer such separation from the Father that He had to cry, "MY GOD, MY GOD, WHY HAVE YOU FORSAKEN ME?"[25] Was that the reason He chose to die such an agonizing death, so that we could have a rigid set of more rules to follow? Was that the good tidings that He intended to preach to the poor, the needy, and the meek? Was that the kind of message that our gracious Savior wanted to bring to His people? More rules and regulations, more laws to follow? More bondage to come under?

I was shocked with the encounter, and I immediately started seeking God about it. As a result, God gave me a dream that night. In the dream, I saw my hairdresser. She had no hair left, only whitish scalp showing that her hair had been burned off. Because the deceived follower had mentioned we couldn't dye our hair, the Lord knew how to get His point across to me—by showing me what such teaching does to someone like my hairdresser, someone whose very employment is to dye hair. Not long after I had the dream, I remember seeking God for the interpretation. I believe it was James 3 that I came across or a scripture carrying a similar interpretation to what we are talking about here. James 3 says that not many of us should become teachers (just what they were mak-

---

[25] Matthew 27:46 AMP.

ing themselves to be), because teachers will be judged with greater severity. And why is that? It is because "we all often stumble and fall and offend in many things."[26] But then here is the verse of interest: "And the tongue is a fire. [The tongue is a] world of wickedness set among our members, contaminating and depraving the whole body and setting on fire the wheel of birth (the cycle of man's nature), being itself ignited by hell (Gehenna)."[27] Through my dream, God was showing me the fruit of "ministries" such as that of the "prophetess" at the convenience store. The words her followers had spoken were like a fire of wickedness. All such a ministry can do is condemn and burn, as what happened to my hairdresser in the dream.

The Bible tells us that what counts in Christianity is faith working through love.[28] It is a true saying that religion will create murderers while Christianity will create martyrs.

New Covenant Versus Old Covenant

The Bible talks about two kinds of righteousness: the righteousness that is of the law (the old covenant) and the righteousness that is of faith in Christ Jesus (the new covenant). Each of them represents a means by which men will attempt to attain righteousness with God.

Now, the apostle Paul is clear in the Word that the law (the old covenant) is not sinful, quite the contrary. Nevertheless, we would not have known what sin was had it not been

---

[26] James 3:2.
[27] James 3:6.
[28] See Galatians 5:6.

for the law.[29] Hence, the law was enacted to make us conscious of sin so that sin may be shown to be exceedingly sinful.[30] And sin being what it is, it found an occasion in the law to make us fall. Because of that, what was meant for good (the law) was used by sin to destroy us; it was used as a sort of forbidden fruit and as a temptation for sin through the weakness of our flesh.[31] This is also why the apostle Paul stated in 1 Corinthians 15:56 KJV that the law is the strength of sin. The law has no power to change our human nature. Another purpose of the law, as explained by the apostle Paul in Galatians 3:24 KJV, was to fulfill the role of a schoolmaster to bring us to Christ that we may be justified by faith. Once the Messiah came, the law was nailed to the cross along with Him and was made obsolete as a means of righteousness to them that believes.[32] His intent in doing so was that His desire concerning us would be fulfilled—His desire being for us to be reconciled with Him through Christ so that we can enjoy a relationship with Him and thus enabled to live in victory and in obedience to Him by His Holy Spirit within us.[33]

Furthermore, we know from the Word and by our own experience that trying to live under the old covenant (the law) doesn't work and that each time we try to submit ourselves to the old code of the letter, it actually works in us the very opposite of what we want it to accomplish in us and ultimately produces fruit unto death.[34] This confirms that if we place ourselves under the law, our failure is assured. All the law

[29] See Romans 7:7.
[30] See Romans 7:13.
[31] See Romans 7:8–14.
[32] See Colossians 2:14; Romans 10:4.
[33] See Ezekiel 36:25–29.
[34] See Romans 7:5, 15–24.

can do for us in the end is to condemn us.[35] This is also why the law is referred to as the dispensation of death, or the ministration of doom.[36] However, if we let go of the old (the letter) and embrace the new (grace), we are truly empowered to live a life of obedience and holiness by the Spirit of God in us. We are therefore placed before a choice; we must choose which way we will trust to make us acceptable to God, the way of the letter or the way of the Spirit of life. One point essential to understand before we make our decision, and which the apostle Paul clearly explained to the church of Galatia, is that the law requires no faith — a very sobering thought given the Bible clearly states that we are justified by faith alone.[37]

We can understand now that each time we submit ourselves back to the old covenant, the law, it can only condemn us because we can't obey it perfectly all the time.[38] However, trusting in the finished work of the cross ministers to us righteousness and life, that is, freedom from condemnation. If you truly want to live for God, but find yourself constantly under heavy condemnation, it is most likely because you are living under old-covenant principles and you are trying to make yourself acceptable to God by keeping some sort of rules, standards, or regulations. They can even be your own made-up rules, or your church's rules, or even the Ten Commandments.

A person living under old-covenant principles reminds me of the way my son Aaron acted sometimes when he was younger. We would give him a warning that he needed to

---

[35] See Galatians 3:10.
[36] See 2 Corinthians 3:6–12 AMPC.
[37] See Galatians 3:12; Galatians 2:16.
[38] See Galatians 3:10.

stop what he was doing or there would be consequences. Our hearts were positive that he would hearken to our warning. Our goal was simply to direct him to choose the right path so that everything would be well with him. In our mind, the negative consequences we listed were not even in the realm of possibility because we expected Aaron to listen and obey. But many times he would cry about the consequences as though he were about to experience them, when, in reality, they were completely theoretical and nonexistent up to that point. Not only that, they were not at all our will for him, and this is why we warned him ahead of time. We didn't even anticipate his choosing the wrong path after we had warned him. But he would ask, crying over the nonexistent consequences, "How long will I not be able to play my game? How long will I not be able to watch TV?" or "How long will I have to stay in my bedroom?"

We would say, "Why do you even ask? Why do you need to study the consequences of disobedience? It is not our intention or our desire for you to experience these consequences. Why do you worry about something that doesn't even exist and that we never intended for you to experience in the first place? We guide you because we want the best for you and because we want you to grow into a fine man of God, the man that God wants you to be. We set boundaries so that you can grow up straight because we have your best interest at heart as well as the hope of a warm, intimate, and peaceful relationship with you as you continue to grow into adulthood. You don't have to not play your game, just do what we tell you. Why do you cry over something that you can avoid so easily? You are not even in that situation; stop crying over it, and obey, and all shall be well with you."

When we establish boundaries for our children, it is not for the sake of ordering them around but always to protect them from greater danger ahead. The same is true of God our heavenly Father toward us His children.

A Christian bound with legalism is a new covenant believer living under fear of the old covenant punishments. Like Aaron was, the legalist is preoccupied with the consequences of sin instead of being focused on the finished work of the cross and the gift to live free from sin. Usually, such a one is unable to enjoy peace with God until he believes that he has reached perfection in his behavior, performance, thoughts, deeds, and actions, which obviously he never reaches. His life is summed up in a quest for perfection, but for the wrong and evil motive to avoid punishment, earn God's acceptance and entrance into heaven instead of because God loves him and because he loves God. For such a one, only perfection can make him feel peaceful and secure.

The legalist believes that she needs to fix herself completely before she can come before God. She believes that she cannot be acceptable to God unless all of her sins have been dealt with through perfect performance. One problem with this picture is that we are incapable of fixing our sin problem. The other problem with this picture is that, like mentioned earlier, it does not require faith. Galatians 3:12 states it plainly: "But the Law does not rest on faith [does not require faith, has nothing to do with faith], for it itself says, He who does them [the things prescribed by the Law] shall live by them [not by faith]." This Scripture was such an eye opener for me when I realized that trying to change myself in my own strength in order to make myself acceptable to God didn't require any faith! It exposed that I was not really living by faith. That troubled me, especially when I considered Galatians 3:11, which states that a man is declared righteous through and by faith. "Now it is evident that no person is justified (declared righteous and brought into right standing with God) through the Law, for the Scripture says, The man in right standing with God [the just, the righteous] shall live by and out of faith and he who through and by faith is declared righteous and in right standing with God shall live."

Let me give you an example. Reading the Bible first thing in the morning can become a law for me. That means that if God asks me one morning to pray through something instead of reading the Word, or if He asks me to work on this book for instance instead of reading the Bible, I will not hearken to the quickening of the Holy Spirit, and I will read the Word instead. Oh, I may appear religious from the outside, but God has rejected my work. God is looking for us to follow His voice, not for us to conform to written (or imagined) laws.[39]

I am sure something like this happens to all of us from time to time; and the more we know Him, the less these scenarios will happen in our lives. But for someone bound with legalism, this sort of situation has become the norm because she has switched her allegiance to what feels safe to follow—religious rules—and has forsaken the leadership of the Lord Himself.

About a year ago, I was talking with a relative and the topic of the baptism of the Holy Spirit and the evidence of speaking in tongues came up in the conversation. I have received the initial baptism of the Holy Spirit and I spoke in

---

[39] See John 10:27.

what appeared to be tongues then, but I have not spoken in tongues since. I am not saying that I will not in the future, but to this day, I have not operated in the gift of tongues. This relative had asked me about speaking in tongues before, and this time he asked again if I spoke in unknown tongues. When I told him that I did not speak in tongues (other than when I received the original baptism), he said that this probably meant that something was wrong in my life, that there probably was a sin of some sort, a blockage. Essentially, there was something that I needed to repent of.

I was careful not to answer anything; I didn't want to defend myself. Instead I looked to God to be my vindicator and thus to vindicate me as He saw fit. While this relative was sharing his thoughts with me, I protected my heart by reminding myself that Christ is my righteousness and that I have been made the righteousness of God through Christ.[40] That night, the Lord gave me a dream. In the dream, God showed me that though this man meant well and though he was zealous for the Lord, what he did that evening was to molest my righteousness. Our faith in Christ is what makes us right with God, and not whether or not we speak in tongues.

Under the new covenant, we have been called to an exciting relationship with the Lord where we are led by the Holy Spirit day by day, moment by moment. The Bible says that as people born of the Spirit of God, we will be like the wind which blows where it wills; and though you hear its sound, you don't know where it comes from nor where it is going.[41] This is why we rightly say that Christianity is relationship with God. Christ also said that if any man will come after

[40] See 1 Corinthians 1:30; 2 Corinthians 5:21.
[41] See John 3:8 AMPC.

Him, let him deny himself, and take up his cross daily, and follow Him.[42] If we need to take up our cross daily and follow Him, it is because He is committed to leading us daily.

Once we have entered into the new covenant, our spirit is perfect (complete), and there is no fixing that needs to occur there. This is where, legally, we have been made right with God freely and immediately the moment we have placed our faith in Jesus Christ for salvation. This is where Christ's righteousness is credited to us on the basis of faith alone. This is what we call *imputed righteousness*. We need to recognize that God has done all that is required to fix us already. All we need do is rest in that finished work and allow the fruit of the Spirit to naturally produce from our knowledge of Him.

Imparted righteousness is where we trust Christ in our weaknesses and struggles to enable us to yield the fruit of the Spirit. It is where we lean on the Holy Spirit for help in our daily lives. Imparted righteousness consists of our progressive and experiential sanctification. It is the righteousness that is worked from the inside out, or in other words, from our spirit, through our soul, and into the realm where people can see. Our imparted righteousness can only happen on the basis of our positional or imputed righteousness through faith in Christ. If we try to overcome our weaknesses, failures, and sin in our own strength, that is, apart from a revelation of who we are in Christ or without an understanding that Christ has already set us free from sin, all we will be left with is the law. The law, that is the old covenant, tells us what we must do and must not do or how we must be, and our only job will be to meet it somehow. But the law will not help us meet it.[43] On

---

[42] See Luke 9:23 KJV.
[43] See Luke 11:46.

the other hand, grace, that is the new covenant, not only will teach us what is right but also will help us do it.[44]

Works Versus Grace

But if it is by grace (His unmerited favor and graciousness), it is no longer conditioned on works or anything men have done. Otherwise, grace would no longer be grace [it would be meaningless].

—Romans 11:6

I believe it was the first year I was born again; the Devil was already working hard at trying to lure me away into legalism. It was a Saturday afternoon, I felt tired and badly wanted to take a nap. But at the same time, the thought of taking a nap instead of reading my Bible made me feel guilty. I was somewhat tormented with this inner battle, and I was so double-minded. *Should I have a nap, or should I read the Bible? If I read the Bible, I am so tired that I will hardly get anything out of it. But if I go to bed and don't read the Bible, am I not keeping from doing what I should be doing on a Saturday afternoon as a Christian? After all, if you have free time, you should be reading the Word, shouldn't you?* O the torment that comes with legalism! Finally, I gave into "the temptation," and I had a nap.

But God is *so good*, I tell you! He is with us at all times, and He sees our struggles. He noticed the struggle and the lie that the Enemy was trying to plant in my soul. And during my nap, God gave me a prophetic dream. The dream was very vivid. I saw many planes hovering in the sky, ready and

---

[44] See Titus 2:12; 2 Peter 1:4; 2 Corinthians 3:6.

waiting for the go-ahead to drop a bomb. They were standing by, waiting for a "yes" to attack or a "no" to retreat. Suddenly, they were given the go-ahead. The answer was "yes" to attack, a bomb was dropped from one of the planes, and I awoke. Although I am not one to follow politics, I knew President George W. Bush was about to make a decision concerning whether he should go ahead and invade Iraq or not. Very soon after I received this dream, he made the decision to invade Iraq and gave the go-ahead; the answer was "yes."

God, in His goodness, gave me a prophetic dream during my nap. He showed me that having a nap was okay with Him, and I didn't need to feel guilty. He wasn't displeased with my choice and all was well.

I believe the reply that the Lord gave Martha when she was busy with much serving will help shine some additional light on the topic at hand:

Now while they were on their way, it occurred that Jesus entered a certain village, and a woman named Martha received and welcomed Him into her house. And she had a sister named Mary, who seated herself at the Lord's feet and was listening to His teaching. But Martha [overly occupied and too busy] was distracted with much serving; and she came up to Him and said, Lord, is it nothing to You that my sister has left me to serve alone? Tell her then to help me [to lend a hand and do her part along with me]! But the Lord replied to her by saying, Martha, Martha, you are anxious and troubled about many things; There is need of only one or but a few things. Mary has chosen the good portion [that which is to her advantage], which shall not be taken away from her.[45]

Are you tired of your walk with God? Do you feel like you are more miserable now as a Christian than you were before Christ came into your life? If that describes you, then it probably means that you have fallen into the trap of legalism—the religion of dead works.[46] "How?" you may ask. By submitting to a set of rules and regulations or some kind of tradition or ritual instead of submitting to God Himself. Sometimes these rules can be self-made; sometimes the religious organization you go to established them. You may even think that it is God imposing them on you. They can literally be the Ten Commandments like I mentioned earlier, or they can be some honorable moral standards that you believe you must somehow live up to— anything you start measuring your performance against, anything you need to do in addition to believing in Christ in order to be saved. Dos and don'ts: don't lust, don't covet, don't steal, witness to every one you come in contact with, do door-to-doors on your days off, fast every week, memorize X number of Bible verses a day, read three chapters of the Bible a day, recite prayers four times a day. You should love more; you need to represent Christ better!

You may not realize it, but because all these requirements are ever before you, you may feel the need to put on a façade and *act* like Christ instead of *be* like Him. Why? Because legalism requires you to be perfect *now*. It leaves you with no other option but to put on a façade before others so if

---

[45] Luke 10:38-42.
[46] See Hebrews 6:1; Hebrews 9:14.

you fail within, at least you won't fail without. What God is after is our heart, and His intent when He saves us is to work a change from the inside out. Legalism will keep us working on the outside because we must perform righteousness perfectly right now, no room for growth, no room for mistakes. Simply put, conducting ourselves like Jesus in our thoughts, deeds, and actions doesn't happen overnight. Therefore, we end up failing miserably when we try to act the part. There we labor in vain, trying to appear what we are not and bearing no real fruit. Plus, we have now added the sin of hypocrisy on top of everything else!

Then again, maybe you are trying to pay for your sins. What do I mean by that? A precious young woman I counselled confessed to me one day that when she sinned she would sometimes sleep on the floor that night as a way to punish herself. But you see, this effort was wasted and all in vain because the only sacrifice for sin which God will ever accept is the sacrifice of His Son Jesus on the cross and nothing else.[47] So if you are trying to pay for your sins, you are wasting your energy doing so. Consider instead that because Jesus paid for our sin and God emptied His wrath onto Jesus, the only acceptable work from you is a sincere heart of repentance which then leads you to confess your sin to God and receive your forgiveness by faith. Therefore, choose to place your trust in the finished work of the cross, in the shed blood of Christ at Calvary. Someone in Christ has been made a new creation and, as such, has received a new heart, a new nature, a new spirit altogether.[48] A healthy Christian has a willing spirit, a yielded spirit toward God, which has all been made

---

[47] See Hebrews 9:22.
[48] See Ezekiel 36:26.

possible through the work at the cross. The flesh remains weak and so does the Christian operating in the flesh.[49] However, in Christ the Christian can do all things.[50] A Christian does not consist of someone who never sins, but of someone whose heart attitude toward God and toward sin has changed. Again, we know from the Word that God immediately forgives us of our sins the moment we confess to Him and cleanses us from all unrighteousness.[51] Trying to pay for our sin is a work of the flesh and appeals to human pride. We are informed in the Word of God that the blood of Christ is the only acceptable payment for our sin because Christ paid our debt in full.[52]

I remember a dream the Lord gave me in my early years as a Christian. I was a young believer then, so I didn't yet know that God didn't only show us positive things about ourselves. It must have taken me two to three months before I brought myself to consider this dream as being from God. In the dream, I was in the bachelor apartment I lived in at the time. I saw a beautiful basket filled with Granny Smith apples. They looked very appetizing. Then I moved on and continued doing the tasks at hand when suddenly I felt hungry. I quickly remembered the apples, so I turned around to take another look, this time with the goal in mind of grabbing one and eating it. However, when I gazed at the apples again, they were all rotten; not even one apple was fresh and good to eat! That was the dream. Through that dream, God was showing me that on the outside, I looked beautiful; but in reality,

---

[49] See Matthew 26:41.
[50] See Philippians 4:13.
[51] See 1 John 1:9.
[52] See Matthew 18:27.

when the rubber hit the road, that is when a true need came and I was hungry, on the inside, there was no real fruit to offer.

The Bible says we will know them by their fruits.[53] For instance, as you take an honest look at your life, you can know whether you are under legalism or not. The fruits of such a life are obvious: you are under a constant sense of guilt and condemnation, you live in fear, and you have no joy, no peace. You try to do good, but it is for the evil motive of protecting yourself from punishment. You always feel like you are falling short. You are usually under the impression that God is displeased with you, and you tend to see God as a harsh, demanding, and exacting perfectionist.

I remember the Lord showing me clearly that, the moment we allow condemnation in our lives, we open the door to the Enemy. This allows the accuser, Satan,[54] to make us believe that something is wrong with us for not having feelings when proper etiquette says that we should have them, or conversely, for having feelings when acceptable manners say we should not have them. Feelings or the lack thereof are no reason to be under condemnation, and if we do not resist the temptation to come under condemnation, we open the door to the Enemy in our lives.

If you are at all like I was, you may believe that you must not have any negative emotions. You may feel the need to suppress them. For instance, if you experience anger, you may fear it and instead of facing it and dealing with it properly, you may end up hiding it.

---

[53] See Matthew 7:20.
[54] See Revelation 12:10.

Maybe temptation disturbs you greatly. And perhaps it is because you confuse temptation with sin. Temptation is not sin. The Bible says that Jesus was tempted in all points and yet He never sinned.[55] I had come to a place where I felt that even temptation was sin. I was such a mess! Can you imagine if temptation is a sin what trouble we would all be in? Not only is someone who lives in such deception hard with themselves, but they will usually have high expectations toward others and will allow little to no room for mistakes in others.

There is a big difference between the change God works from the inside (grace) and the change legalism works from the outside (our works). Legalism causes us to try to obey in order to protect ourselves from harm, from disapproval, and to exalt ourselves by making ourselves acceptable to God. On the other hand, when we allow God to change us from the inside, we serve Him because we love Him, and "we love Him because He first loved us."[56] We want to be good witnesses, because we love Him and we want to glorify Him. We also increasingly care for souls. Each day we seek His leading and we seek to follow Him. We don't want to sin, because we love righteousness and we hate sin, not because we are afraid of hell or of God's rejecting us. We know we are accepted through Christ, and this very fact purifies our motives so that all that is left is faith working by love.[57]

Furthermore, legalism makes us feel we have not done enough. How can we really know that we have met all of God's expectations in an area? The problem is, when under the law, we are never really sure if we have done enough.

---

[55] See Matthew 4:1; Hebrews 4:15 KJV.
[56] 1 John 4:19.
[57] See Galatians 5:6.

Remember, the Bible says that if we are trying to be justified by the law, we need to meet the entire law.[58] Just like Derek Prince said in his book, "We must realize that keeping a little bit of the law some of the time does not do us any good. If we are going to be justified by keeping the law, we have to keep the whole law all the time."[59]

Legalism can also express itself through an unbalanced fear of not having an infallible doctrine. You may fear that if you don't have a spotless doctrine you are at risk of going to hell. The danger is that one day you will wake up and find you have placed your faith in a doctrine instead of in Christ. Please don't misunderstand me; sound doctrine is essential because it will make the difference as to whether we are in the truth or not. What I am talking about here is when we begin to lose our peace over some unanswered doctrinal questions. Children of God should abide in peace regardless of whether they have it all figured out or not. Therefore, we need to be able to have peace in Christ and trust Him to lead us into all truth.[60]

Do you see a common thread that accompanies legalism (trying to please God through works)? Legalism is fueled by fear. Fear is selfish and the one who fears seeks only to protect oneself. It is therefore the opposite of giving. Fear is one of the main spirits through which Satan gains entrance into our lives; faith is the door through which God works in our lives. Fear is the opposite of faith and love, the fruit that the grace of Christ brings. We are called to reverently fear the

---

[58] See James 2:10.

[59] Prince, *Lucifer Exposed*, 81–82.

[60] I elaborate on this in chapter 4, under the section "The Only Voice That Makes the Difference."

Lord but not to be afraid of Him, and there is a difference. A believer who is habitually living in fear is no longer living the Spirit-led life that God has intended for him or her to walk in. I learn a lot from the mistakes that I make. If I am afraid to make mistakes, then I will never be able to grow because the fear attached to those mistakes will paralyze all growth and will bind me to my mistakes. However, if I am free to be imperfect, I will grow and learn from my mistakes. The love of God will foster genuine growth in my life. Plus my mistakes help keep me humble. I have come to realize that without my slipups, I personally wouldn't be able to extend mercy to others.

When I was living under legalism, I found myself in a constant state of introspection, keeping a close eye on all of my heart motives for fear that something may be wrong with me. Now, it is very good to keep a close eye on our heart motives, and the Bible tells us to do so.[61] We must guard our hearts with all diligence, for out of our hearts flow the issues of life.[62] However, I was serving God out of the wrong heart; I was doing it to keep my salvation. I was doing it so that God would not judge me and sentence me to hell if something was wrong with my heart's motives. I was afraid that one thought, one feeling, one motive was enough to send me to hell if I died that very moment. My righteousness was found in a set of rules. Such are evil motives. They are self-centered motives. They are motives stemming from someone who does not obey the gospel, that is, from someone who does not trust Christ with their soul. We have been saved so that we can desire holiness out of a pure heart, out of a love for holiness, and out of

[61] See 1 Corinthians 11:28.
[62] See Proverbs 4:23 KJV.

a love for God Himself. We are not to be constantly motivated because we are afraid of God and hell. Something is wrong if that is the driving force in our lives.

When we are in Christ, we no longer feel condemned when we sin; instead we feel grieved, and there is a big difference! Moreover, when our faith is in the finished work of the cross, God is able to show us mercy even when we fall short. When we submit ourselves to the law, however, there is no room for mercy there. That is why the apostle Paul said that those under the law are under a curse;[63] we simply can't do it perfectly, which can only mean that the natural ending for anyone seeking to be justified through obeying the law is condemnation and death. However, if we will come under grace, there the blood of Christ cries out, "Mercy!" for those whose hearts were changed at Calvary.[64] Can you see it? This is why Christ could say about the tax collector who cried out for mercy, "I tell you, this man went down to his house justified."[65] However, He couldn't draw the same conclusion about the self-righteous man who was busy comparing himself with the tax collector.[66]

Jesus said the merciful are blessed, because they will be shown mercy.[67] James said that no mercy will be shown to the merciless.[68] Do you know what that tells me? That tells me that we *all* need mercy, which in turn can only mean that no one is perfect or we wouldn't need mercy. Therefore, submitting to the law is sure failure. We might as well humble our-

---

[63] See Galatians 3:10.
[64] See Hebrews 12:24.
[65] Luke 18:14 KJV.
[66] See Luke 18:11–12.
[67] See Matthew 5:7.
[68] See James 2:13.

selves and submit to Christ and place ourselves under His grace.

I love what John Ortberg says, and though I may not have the exact words, I believe I captured the spirit of what I heard him say one day: it is not about trying but training. How good that is! He went on to explain that trying to love more when we know we are falling short would be the same as someone out of shape trying to run a marathon. We just can't. In essence, the idea was that if we want to love more, we need to begin to exercise our faith to do unto others what we would like them to do unto us until we have grown to the place of maturity in the area of love so the love of Christ controls our hearts.[69] And so on and so forth.

I was prominently legalistic toward myself. And that is what confused me the most at first. I said, "How can this be? How can I be legalistic? I minister grace to others." And so I did indeed. I did display a lot of grace and mercy toward others, but I wouldn't receive the same mercy for myself. I do believe, however, that I was legalistic toward my husband, because I remember looking at everything that he wasn't doing and should be doing, and vice versa, and grumbling under my breath at how terrible it was for him to be the way that he was. I also made sure to let him know what he needed to do more or conversely, what he needed to stop doing. It is much easier to have these kinds of expectations toward the ones nearest to us.

As people of God, we will have discernment, and God can allow us to notice when people miss the mark in an area at times. But our heart should be a heart of compassion, pity,

---

[69] See 2 Corinthians 5:14.

and love and not a heart filled with judgment and contempt. If God shows us anything about someone else, it is for the purpose of praying for them and not for condemning them. What I should have done instead of despising my husband is feel sorry for him, pray for him in love, and allow myself to overlook his transgression every once in a while[70]—loving him into wholeness as opposed to nagging him into madness!

Another thing the Lord began to show me was the critical roles that praying from my heart, worshipping from my heart, and speaking from my heart play in this spiritual warfare. These are significant defenses against legalism.

Isaiah 29:13 describes a people whose relationship with God is reduced to ritualism, going through the motions, and following a set of rules and regulations. "And the Lord said, Forasmuch as this people draw near Me with their mouth and honor Me with their lips but remove their hearts and minds far from Me, and their fear and reverence for Me are a commandment of men that is learned by repetition [without any thought as to the meaning]."

This may seem strange to you, but serving the Lord from our hearts helps *us* know what we really stand for, and it does a work within us. If we only speak from our lips, we may not be consciously aware of it, but our inner man knows that we do not really mean what we say. It opens the door for further double-mindedness in our lives, not knowing who we really love, who we really serve, and what we really believe. When we begin to mean what we say and say what we mean, it strengthens our understanding of our position in God; it helps drive out double-mindedness and replace it with single-

[70] See Proverbs 17:9.

mindedness. Once our hearts are involved, we become more and more secure in Him because we know what we believe. When our whole hearts are in it, we will have confidence before God, and peace will flood our hearts as double-mindedness is defeated in our lives.[71]

James 4:8 says this: "Come close to God and He will come close to you. [Recognize that you are] sinners, get your soiled hands clean; [realize that you have been disloyal] wavering individuals with divided interests, and purify your hearts [of your spiritual adultery]."

You may be afraid of being hurt or disappointed, so you don't allow your heart to believe fully in God, in God's grace, or to have a heartfelt relationship with the Lord. Maybe you are afraid that what you allow yourself to believe won't happen. It could be you do not serve God from the heart because it demands an additional effort on your part as opposed to going through the motions and offering Him only your works. It does require an effort on our part to walk by faith and not by sight, to receive acceptance based on His work of grace and not based on our works of the flesh. It is hard sometimes to trust God and not take matters into our own hands. But the price of walking in the flesh is too high and the yoke is too great to carry. Jesus said to come to Him if we labor and are heavy laden and He will give us rest. He told us to learn of Him, for He is meek and lowly in heart. He will give us rest for our souls; His burden is light and His yoke is easy.[72] Serving God from our hearts while relying fully on His grace will give us rest for our soul. However, trying to obey a set of

---

[71] See 1 John 3:21.
[72] See Matthew 11:28–30 KJV.

rules in order to please God with our works will burden us until we are completely worn out.

The Antidote

The difference between legalism and grace is that legalism causes one to serve God in order to get saved or stay saved, while grace causes one to serve God *because* one is saved.

A legalist navigates his life around his attempt to perform the Christian faith perfectly by complying with rules and regulations. The things he thinks about the most have become that code of conduct that he must comply with, that level of holiness that he must reach in order to stay out of trouble, that sin that he must overcome or he is doomed, the sins that are seemingly ever present with him and need to be removed, and his doctrine which must be spotless if he wants to be safe. He wants to be holy for fear of punishment. Knowing the Lord is no longer the central focus of his life; it is no longer the joy of a sweet fellowship with his loving Lord that dominates his thoughts and heart, but rather a dreadful feeling that he is just not measuring up.

On the other hand, the Christian under grace longs for holiness because he is hungry for righteousness and because his new nature hates sin.[73] He navigates his life around Jesus' finished work at the cross. He seeks to please God because he loves God and because God loves him. His desire to glorify God is what motivates his behavior, his actions and his reactions.

---

[73] See Proverbs 8:13; 1 John 3:9.

The law was not made for the righteous man, but for the lawless and disobedient.[74] As to the one who has been made right with God through his faith in Jesus Christ, the law is written on his heart.[75] So legalism teaches another gospel, because it teaches something other than Christ and Christ crucified as a means of righteousness; legalism is a religion of dead works and becomes a deadly poison to those who embrace it. See again within its context what the apostle Paul says: "But I fear, lest by any means, as the serpent beguiled Eve through his subtlety, so your minds should be corrupted from the simplicity that is in Christ."[76] The *Amplified Bible, Classic Edition* puts it this way: "But [now] I am fearful, lest that even as the serpent beguiled Eve by his cunning, so your minds may be corrupted and seduced from wholehearted and sincere and pure devotion to Christ." Legalism does just that; it corrupts our minds so we no longer have the finished work of the cross as the source of our hope; it entices us to another. On the other hand, the pure gospel of Jesus Christ, in its simplicity, produces in us an undivided, wholehearted, pure devotion to Christ. If you have been poisoned by the spirit of legalism, God's unfailing grace is your antidote.

***

Religion is the worse form of slavery to ever afflict mankind.

—C. M. Ward

---

[74] See 1 Timothy 1:9 KJV.
[75] See Jeremiah 31:33.
[76] 2 Corinthians 11:3 KJV.

CHAPTER 3
THE ROOTS OF LEGALISM

Rebellion

Rebellion is as the sin of witchcraft, and stubbornness is as iniquity and idolatry.

—1 Samuel 15:23a

We need to go in the proper order. First we need to make sure that we have chosen Jesus as the Lord of our lives. Once this is settled, then we are ready to build on top of this foundation. It sounds simple and one may say, of course, Jesus is the Lord of my life! However, like we have learned in chapter 2, when one is bound by legalism, it means there is rebellion in his life because an illegitimate authority is present. Again, legalism is very subtle and operates in the dark so much so that the one under its spell doesn't even realize what is really happening.

We have learned that witchcraft is the evil power that obscures the revelation of the cross in the legalist's life. In 1 Samuel 15:23, we are told that the sin of witchcraft can be paralleled to the sin of rebellion. Therefore, if witchcraft was my problem, rebellion was my problem also. In order to be delivered from legalism, I needed to be delivered from the root of rebellion. If you are still not sure, let's take another look at Galatians 3:1. But this time let's read it from the King James Version, as this version gives us another perspective. "O foolish Galatians, who hath bewitched you, that ye should not *obey* the truth, before whose eyes Jesus Christ hath been evidently set forth, crucified among you?"[1]

We see here that the apostle Paul describes not believing the truth about Christ crucified as disobedience. Therefore, if we believe the message, we are regarded as obedient; but if we won't believe, we are regarded as rebellious.

A Christian is someone who agrees to completely submit to the leadership of the Holy Spirit. I was shocked when I realized that even after the Lord had revealed to me that legalism was my problem, there was that in me which had a really hard time simply surrendering to Jesus and coming back to Him. It was difficult to make Him my Lord again. I had been in excruciating torment day and night; but to my amazement, when it came time to surrender again to Him, I found myself struggling greatly to do so. It was hard to bow before Christ and to place myself under His authority. I tried so hard to finally yield. And sometimes that is exactly it; we need to have tried so hard by ourselves that we finally reach the end of our rope and surrender.

I was wondering when I was ever going to give up resisting His authority. How low did I need to go and how bad did it need to get for me to surrender? The Lord in His goodness helped me in my struggle by leading me to Jeremiah 3:22 KJV: "Return, ye backsliding children, and I will heal your backslidings." I depended a lot on this Scripture and His promise that if I only returned to Him, He would take care of purging me from the rebellion that was in me. This Scripture was one of the main Scriptures God used to enable me to turn around and take the first step toward Him again. This Scrip-

---

[1] Galatians 3:1 KJV, emphasis added.

ture let me know that as long as I had the desire to come back (that I was repentant) and that as long as I trusted Him to deliver me from rebellion, He would do in me what I couldn't do—change my heart and transform it from a hardened and rebellious heart to a humble and submissive one.

> And I will give them one heart [a new heart] and I will put a new spirit within them; and I will take the stony [unnaturally hardened] heart out of their flesh, and will give them a heart of flesh [sensitive and responsive to the touch of their God], That they may walk in My statutes and keep My ordinances, and do them. And they shall be My people, and I will be their God. But as for those whose heart yearns for and goes after their detestable things and their loathsome abominations [associated with idolatry], I will repay their deeds upon their own heads, says the Lord God.
>
> —Ezekiel 11:19–21

We can trust that through His work at Calvary He has given us every provision that we need to be set free and delivered from rebellion. We can trust Him to work in us a heart that is tender to the touch of our Master.

Matthew 6:24 became especially relevant for me during that time. Jesus says: "No one can serve two masters; for either he will hate the one and love the other, or he will stand by and be devoted to the one and despise and be against the other. You cannot serve God and mammon (deceitful riches, money, possessions, or whatever is trusted in)."

81

Of course, I was not debating between God and money, but the principle was nevertheless the same; I was debating between making Jesus my master and submitting to Him wholeheartedly or making myself my own lord and attempting to make myself righteous independently of God. The Bible tells us not to fear them which kill the body, but are not able to kill the soul; but rather fear him which is able to destroy both soul and body in hell.[2]

After wrestling with God for control, I can assure you that the Lord is stronger than we are and that we are truly helpless before Him. God will not bend, but He will help us bend if we ask Him to. The only way to peace is to surrender, because God is mightier than we are. We need to approach Him from a standpoint of humility, brokenness, and contriteness of heart. You and I are truly vulnerable before Him, and He has the last word in the matter. When it's all said and done, we are at His mercy. We are at His mercy, and we need to surrender to this fact or we will never have peace. Christianity is total surrender and submission to the Holy Spirit's leading and is therefore entirely supernatural. As long as we cooperate with Him and partner with Him, He will lead us all the way to the finish line.

Studying Jesus' nature is really helpful when it comes to ridding ourselves of rebellion. Jesus is our leader, and He does lead by example. Therefore, what also helped me was to meditate on Scriptures that highlighted His servant's heart, His meekness, and His love. The following Scriptures are ex-

---

[2] See Matthew 10:28 KJV.

amples of that.[3] Please take the time to read them and to discover how humble our own Master is:

I am able to do nothing from Myself [independently, of My own accord—but only as I am taught by God and as I get His orders]. Even as I hear, I judge [I decide as I am bidden to decide. As the voice comes to Me, so I give a decision], and My judgment is right (just, righteous), because I do not seek or consult My own will [I have no desire to do what is pleasing to Myself, My own aim, My own purpose] but only the will and pleasure of the Father Who sent Me.

—John 5:30

Although He was a Son, He learned [active, special] obedience through what He suffered. And, [His completed experience] making Him perfectly [equipped], He became the Author and Source of eternal salvation to all those who give heed and obey Him.

—Hebrews 5:8–9

And be like men who are waiting for their master to return home from the marriage feast, so that when he returns from the wedding and comes and knocks, they may open to him immediately. Blessed (happy, fortunate, and to be envied) are those servants whom the master

---

[3] You can also refer to Philippians 2:5–10 and Matthew 11:28–30 for more Scriptures on this topic.

finds awake and alert and watching when he
comes. Truly I say to you, he will gird himself
and have them recline at table and will come
and serve them! If he comes in the second watch
(before midnight) or the third watch (after midnight), and finds them so, blessed (happy, fortunate, and to be envied) are those servants!

—Luke 12:36–38

Luke 12:37 particularly blesses my heart. Did you read
that? Jesus Himself will recline at the table and serve us! He is
so confident in who He is, He is so humble and He loves us so
much that serving us does not bother Him. Therefore, we
never need to be concerned that His heart is not right toward
us. No, His motives are pure toward us. He loves us so much,
and we can trust wholeheartedly that He always has our best
interest at heart and that He is not self-seeking. He has a servant's heart. He is the humblest person there is. There is no
pride in Him. He is love.[4] The same can be true of us, His
saints. If we know who we are in Christ, it will not be belit-
tling to us to serve Him or to serve one another. I love Him
and others because He first loved me.[5] I serve Him and others
because He first served me.

How we see God is vitally important for a sound belief
system and for a healthy relationship with Him. I love how
the *Amplified Bible, Classic Edition* describes what faith is in 2
Timothy 1:5: "the leaning of your entire personality on God in
Christ in absolute trust and confidence in His power, wisdom,
and goodness." It is of utmost importance to know Him and

[4] See 1 John 4:8.
[5] See 1 John 4:19.

to know His nature; for if we do not have the proper picture of who God is and of His nature, defeat will sooner or later be our portion. We must make it a priority to study to know Him, or our relationship with the Lord will be greatly hindered through lack of knowledge. As I was seeking freedom in that area, I very quickly realized that the way I saw Him was going to play a monumental role in setting me free and keeping me free from rebellion.

We are coheirs with Christ.[6] He gave us everything. The Bible tells us in 1 John 3:2 that we will be like Him, which means that He holds nothing back from us. It pleased Him to give us the kingdom.[7] We lack no good thing, for no good thing will He withhold from the ones who walk uprightly.[8] And we will reign with Him for eternity.[9]

Somebody has to be in charge, and whether we like it or not, we do need authority in our lives. We need to be loved by a father; we need to be cared for by a shepherd. And He can do all of this because He cannot be tempted with evil.[10] Therefore, we can rest secure in His love and motives toward us always. In Him there is no shadow of turning.[11] He is always just, even when we don't understand with our minds; and we can trust with our hearts that He is always doing what is right.

Giving Him all the glory is the right thing to do because He does deserve all the glory, and He said in His Word

---

[6] See Romans 8:17.
[7] See Luke 12:32.
[8] See Psalm 84:11.
[9] See 2 Timothy 2:12.
[10] See James 1:13 KJV.
[11] See James 1:17 KJV.

that He will not share His glory with anyone.[12] He also said that no flesh will glory in His presence.[13] Moreover, giving God His due glory protects us from pride, the very sin that caused Lucifer to fall. "Your heart was lifted up because of your beauty; you corrupted your wisdom for the sake of your splendor."[14] Lucifer's pride caused his downfall. What Satan has done by wanting to become like God, be worshipped and be in authority and be in control is wrong. This plan could have only opened the door for disagreement and for war. Consider what happens if you have two rulers who won't come into agreement. Confusion, disorder, and chaos. If Lucifer was already blessed beyond measure, why would he still want to be the supreme ruler? The only reason is for self-seeking and self-exalting motives, and it ultimately caused his fall.[15]

The spirit of rebellion is the spirit of the antichrist so we want to resist it at all costs. Christ completely submitted Himself to the Father, and the Father gave Him all authority as a result. The Bible says that when all things are subdued unto Christ, then He will also Himself be subject unto the Father that God may be all in all.[16] After all, doesn't Jesus deserve to be the one in highest authority given He is the one who died for us not to mention that He is God the Son?

We need to know and experience His love for ourselves, and out of that loving relationship we will naturally want to please Him and submit to Him. Ephesians 3:16–21 is a

---

[12] See Isaiah 42:8.
[13] See 1 Corinthians 1:29 KJV.
[14] Ezekiel 28:17 NKJV.
[15] See Isaiah 14:12.
[16] See 1 Corinthians 15:28 KJV.

great place to start. Just like good parents will not have children for the sake of controlling them, but instead for the sake of love, intimacy, and fellowship, God also gave birth to us for the sake of love, intimacy, and fellowship. He has our best interests at heart. However, if we do not know the intense love God has for us, we will likely be prone to resist His authority in our life and attempt to please him by submitting to rules and laws. Submitting to a law is just another way to run from God's authority, because the law serves as a middleman between God and us. There, we are still in control of our own lives, for like we have learned already, the law is not based on faith nor does it require any trust in God.[17] So a lack of willing submission is likely to come from a lack of revelation of God's love. The Bible says that we love Him because He first loved us; and when we love Him, the automatic and natural response will be to obey Him.[18] Isaiah 48:17 NIV also helped me understand what I am sharing with you here, which is that He is leading us for our benefit. "This is what the LORD says—your Redeemer, the Holy One of Israel: 'I am the LORD your God, who teaches you what is best for you, who directs you in the way you should go.'"

It is prideful to think that we can manage our own life. We need a leader, and Jesus is that leader. We also need to understand what we really are without Him; dead in trespasses and sin.[19] See how Jesus responded when He saw people without a leader. Hear the cry of His heart and the true motive behind that cry in this Scripture. "When He saw the throngs, He was moved with pity and sympathy for them, be-

---

[17] See Galatians 3:12.
[18] See 1 John 4:19; John 14:23.
[19] See Ephesians 2:1 KJV.

cause they were bewildered (harassed and distressed and dejected and helpless), like sheep without a shepherd."[20]

We need to understand what we really are, sheep, and not let pride blind us to our need for His authority in our lives. Sheep are lost without a shepherd. Sheep are very dependent. Sheep are known as dumb beasts! A very humbling thought isn't it? As sheep, we need to constantly seek our Shepherd's guidance and provision for each day's needs. And what is His heart toward us, His sheep? Well, read again this part of verse 36 from Matthew chapter 9: "He was moved with pity and sympathy for them." His heart is filled with love for us, *His* sheep. We are His treasured possession, purchased by His very own blood.[21] We are valuable to Him, and the cross and His Word should be sufficient proof to us of this.

We need a father, for we are but children in this life.[22] We need a father to protect, guide, and defend us. We need His attention, His care, and His chastisement to be a whole person. We need His leading, and we need to follow Him. Not only because He is God, but for our best interest also.

What about worship? Rebellion will create a reluctance to worship. However, the Bible mentions that we are called to worship Him in spirit and in truth.[23] We bow down before Him out of great love, out of intimacy with Him. Just like we have intimacy with our spouse, we have intimacy with God through worship and through submission. Doesn't the Bible say in Romans 12:1 that making a decisive dedication of our

---

[20] Matthew 9:36.
[21] See 1 Corinthians 6:20.
[22] See 1 John 2:1.
[23] See John 4:23–24.

bodies (presenting all your members and faculties) as a living sacrifice, holy (devoted, consecrated) and well pleasing to God, is our reasonable (rational, intelligent) service and spiritual worship? So our intimacy with God is expressed through our obedience to Him and our humble submission is like giving ourselves to Him just like we give ourselves to our spouse. When we give ourselves to God in this way, the result is peace that passes understanding.

I would have to say that peace is what I have longed for the most in my life. Undoubtedly, the reason for this is because I have known the extreme torment and anxiety that came along with trying to submit to the law. I like what Beth Moore says in referring to Isaiah 9:6–7 in her powerful book *Breaking Free*: "Isaiah 9:6–7 perfectly portrays the key to peace: authority. When we allow the Prince of Peace to govern our lives, peace either immediately or ultimately results. Peace accompanies authority."[24]

> For to us a Child is born, to us a Son is given; and the government shall be upon His shoulder, and His name shall be called Wonderful Counselor, Mighty God, Everlasting Father [of Eternity], Prince of Peace. Of the increase of His government and of peace there shall be no end, upon the throne of David and over his kingdom, to establish it and to uphold it with justice and with righteousness from the [latter] time forth, even forevermore. The zeal of the Lord of hosts will perform this.
>
> —Isaiah 9:6–7

---

[24] Moore, *Breaking Free*, 42.

I remember Advika sharing with me something the Lord had spoken to her: "Relinquish all control." The funny part is that she had to look up the word *relinquish* because she didn't even know what the word meant. What God was asking her to do was willingly surrender all control to Him and yield herself entirely to Him in every area of her life. He is asking the same of all of us. One important element of our freedom from rebellion is the need to know our purpose, our function. Why did God create us? What was God's purpose in creating us? If there were a manual attached to us human beings, what would it say? I believe we can find it in Ecclesiastes 12:13: "All has been heard; the end of the matter is: Fear God [revere and worship Him, knowing that He is] and keep His commandments, for this is the whole of man [the full, original purpose of his creation, the object of God's providence, the root of character, the foundation of all happiness, the adjustment to all inharmonious circumstances and conditions under the sun] and the whole [duty] for every man." And 1 John 3:23 helps us understand the full meaning of Ecclesiastes 12:13 according to the new covenant: "And this is His order (His command, His injunction): that we should believe in (put our faith and trust in and adhere to and rely on) the name of His Son Jesus Christ (the Messiah), and that we should love one another, just as He has commanded us."

In light of the above, let us therefore pray like David prayed in Psalm 51:10 KJV: "Create in me a clean heart, O God; and renew a right spirit within me."

Doubt and Unbelief

Fight the good fight of the faith; lay hold of the eternal life to which you were summoned and [for which] you confessed the good confession [of faith] before many witnesses.

—1 Timothy 6:12

To have doubt is very troubling and unsettling. As a born-again believer, to have doubt is to be divided, to be double-minded. Nothing will steal your peace more than being double-minded. But God wants to help us overcome it also. We may think that we believe from the heart; but for me, after God showed me I was under the spell of legalism, I also had the painful realization that I was no longer close to the Lord from the heart. My heart was far from Him. It had been filled with so much fear that there was very little place left for faith and for the love of God. I knew that I had to come back, *with my heart*. I had to truly believe from the heart and trust God that He would take care of me.

It takes faith to believe that the Lord will lead us into the path of righteousness moment by moment. Will He really come through for me if I let go of all control and let Him keep me and guide me? Will He really warn me when I am about to do something that I shouldn't do? Will He show me mercy if I fail? It is much easier to have a law created: I shall not covet, I shall not be proud, and I shall not lie. That allows me to remain in control instead of trusting God with my soul. When we find ourselves wrapped up in the torment that is caused by legalism, it is because we do not understand repentance

91

nor do we have the revelation that righteousness is first and foremost a condition of the heart.[25]

When we have little to no faith, all we have left is religion. Religion is going through the motions. It is the place where our faith has become mostly mental—head knowledge. I have myself chosen religious paths when plagued with doubts and unbelief. A couple of years before I fell deep into legalism, God spoke to me these words: "Do not look to the left nor to the right, but focus on God." I am sorry to say that I did not hearken to the warning, and I allowed myself to dive deeper and deeper into the different theories and reasonings that came into my mind. Over time, it caused me extreme anxiety and double-mindedness and bore only fruit unto death. The solution never is to analyze the Enemy's reasoning to see if there is some ground in it after all, but the solution always is to seek God for revelation knowledge in the areas where we experience confusion.

In my early walk with God, I remember struggling with doubts. I really believed in my heart, but I had nagging doubts that would attack my mind. I knew from the Word it was essential that I guard my heart with all diligence.[26] I prayed about the doubts I had for quite some time. I thought surely I couldn't just continue to call myself a Christian if I had doubts. Didn't that make me a hypocrite, saying that I was a Christian, proclaiming Christ, and yet behind the scenes doubting the faith that I professed? This led me to consider leaving the faith. One evening, I felt the prompting of the Holy Spirit within me to pick up a book, *The Case for Faith*, written by Lee Strobel, which was sitting on my night table. I said,

---

[25] This is discussed in more detail in chapter 4.
[26] See Proverbs 4:23.

"Bah, I don't feel like reading that book tonight. I didn't really plan to read that book tonight." However, I felt this insistent prompting. So I said something like, "Okay, okay! I will open it, but I don't even know where to look. This is a fairly big book. How am I supposed to know what to read?"

I decided to go to the table of contents and read through the list of chapters to see if something stood out. As I read through each chapter title, I landed on one named "I Still Have Doubts, so I Can't Be a Christian." I knew right away what God was saying. He was telling me that I could still be a Christian even if I had some doubts! So I went right ahead and read what the author had to say in that chapter. Can you imagine the tragedy had I left the faith because of some doubts? No matter what you are going through, God can see you through. You only need to stay in the program, place your trust in Him; He is well able to deliver you even from nagging doubts and unbelief. Only give Him some time to work in your life; He knows what He is doing.

In trying to believe with our own strength, we are still in the works of the flesh and we are still showing independence from God. Christianity is supernatural from the very beginning to the very end. It is true that Christianity excludes all boasting.[27] I have come to realize that if I want to stand and remain standing, I need to trust Christ in everything and for everything. If there are any areas whatsoever where I still trust in my own strength and my own ability, sooner or later, I will fall under the pressure; and whatever I have built will crumble under the trial. The only way that my house can

---

[27] See Romans 3:27.

stand is if it is safely secured and founded on the Rock who is Jesus, and His Word.[28]

I have come to understand that this principle even applies to my ability to believe. One day, I was standing in my home office inquiring of the Lord about Hebrews 12:2, which essentially says that Jesus is the Author and Finisher of our faith. I knew that different versions of the Bible translated this passage differently. I wanted it to mean that Jesus was the Author, the Enabler, the Provider, the Sustainer, the Helper and the Finisher of my faith. I was tired of fearing to lose my faith. I was tired of trying to keep my faith in my own strength. I needed to know that I could rely on someone, something more stable and more powerful than I was in the area of my faith, and really, in every area that concerned me. Suddenly, as I was seeking God on that Scripture, I sensed how supernatural Christianity really is. It didn't last long. But for a brief moment, I believe the Lord allowed me to recognize how supernatural our faith is, how it is of the Spirit of God, and how it does not, nor can it, originate from ourselves apart from Him.

I need to depend on Him even to help my faith. I need to build my house on Him as the source of my faith. And I depend on Him to be my faith Provider, my faith Sustainer, and my faith Enabler. I have come to realize that if I want my house to stand no matter what comes against me, I need to build it on Him, through Him, and by His might from the very foundation to the very finishing touch.

Have you ever stopped to think that if you are afraid that you don't have faith, it is *because* you do have faith? Only

---

[28] See Matthew 7:24–27.

someone who really believes and knows for themselves that we are saved through faith alone can understand the danger of not having such faith. That has got to mean that we believe or we would not fear to lose what we already have. I have at times pondered on that thought myself; isn't it ridiculous how the Devil can torment us, and how torment makes no sense?

We cannot believe by our own strength. And the Bible confirms that by saying that faith comes by hearing and hearing by the Word of God.[29] If you struggle with doubt and unbelief, make sure to spend quality time in the Word of God. Be consistent. You need to mean business. Not only that, but make sure to ask God to open your understanding to the Word you are reading. We need the Holy Spirit to give us revelation concerning the Scriptures. According to Matthew 16:13–17, knowing who Jesus is comes from revelation knowledge given by the Father through His Holy Spirit:

> Now when Jesus went into the region of Caesarea Philippi, He asked His disciples, who do people say that the Son of Man is? And they answered, some say John the Baptist; others say Elijah; and others Jeremiah or one of the prophets. He said to them, but who do you [yourselves] say that I am? Simon Peter replied, you are the Christ, the Son of the living God. Then Jesus answered him, blessed (happy, fortunate, and to be envied) are you, Simon Bar-Jonah. For flesh and blood [men] have not revealed this to you, but My Father Who is in heaven.[30]

---

[29] See Romans 10:17 NKJV.
[30] Matthew 16:13–17.

As we can see from this Scripture and others, it is God the Father Himself who draws us to Jesus by His Holy Spirit and who opens our spiritual eyes and our spiritual understanding, which in turn causes us to believe.[31] Without revelation from God, we cannot believe in Christ. Therefore, if you are trying to fight your doubts and convince yourself through human reasoning, you will fail. Again, only God can enable you by His Spirit.

The Bible says, "Today, if you would hear His voice and when you hear it, do not harden your hearts."[32] It is also important to understand that underneath faith ultimately is the choice to believe; and underneath unbelief ultimately is the choice not to believe. God draws us by His Spirit and provides the revelation and the faith that we need to come to Christ. With our free will we can either choose to yield to the moving of the Holy Spirit in our lives or we can harden our hearts and refuse His wooing. For some, miracles will be sufficient for them to settle all doubts, because they believe in their heart that a miracle performed by Jesus is a reasonable proof of who Jesus is.[33] But for others, nothing Jesus does changes their beliefs, because something deeper is going on. Hebrews 4:2 says that the message they heard did not benefit them, because it was not mixed with faith (with the leaning of the entire personality on God in absolute trust and confidence in His power, wisdom, and goodness) by those who heard it. That is why it is important when struggling with doubts and unbelief to, as contradictory as it may sound, seek God about them and ask Him to deliver us. Asking God for help is us

---

[31] See John 6:44.
[32] See Hebrews 4:7.
[33] See John 2:23; Matthew 11:23.

"choosing" to believe, although we cannot do the believing on our own without His help. Look at the man whose son was possessed by a foul spirit in Mark 9:24 KJV, and see how he dealt with his doubts: "And straightway the father of the child cried out, and said with tears, Lord, I believe; help thou mine unbelief." We need only to do the same; we need only to ask Jesus: "Lord I believe, help my unbelief!" And you can rest assured that He will, every time.

I was driving one afternoon to a worship practice. On my way there, I pondered again how I first got saved: with childlike faith. There were no miracles, no apparitions, no signs, no crises in my life, but just a choice to believe. How did I know I had the truth? Simple. Peace and joy flooded my soul; Christ came and took residence within my heart. We know we have the truth for the simple fact that the Spirit of God bears witness with our spirit that we are children of God.[34] So in order to get rid of my doubts, I didn't need more miracles, more signs, etc., just like I didn't need all of these things when I was born again. The way that I was saved was the same way that I would walk my Christian walk; and that is with simple, childlike faith. Jesus said that the kingdom of God is within us.[35] And the apostle Paul said that we are seated in heavenly places even now.[36]

I remember seeking God regarding the doubts that I was periodically struggling with throughout my Christian walk. On one particular occasion, after praying quite earnestly for about two to three months, the Lord spoke to me one night in a dream and said these life-changing words: "It takes time

---

[34] See Romans 8:16 NKJV.
[35] See Luke 17:21.
[36] See Ephesians 2:6.

to go from faith to conviction, and God is patient." The amazing thing about these words was that my main prayer had been: "Lord convince me!" The fact that God used the word *conviction* (which means the state of being convinced) instead of the word *faith* really ministered to me. Romans 1:17 KJV should help shine more light on God's statement to me that night. "For therein is the righteousness of God revealed from faith to faith: as it is written, The just shall live by faith."[37]

Now if I experience doubts in an area, or if I do not feel as convinced as I wish I'd be, I remember these words and no longer feel condemned about it. It doesn't mean that I am not in the faith, nor does it necessarily mean that I have no faith; but instead, I am already in the faith, and I need my faith to grow from faith to conviction. So I pray to God to increase my faith, to strengthen my faith, and to convince me in the area of need; and He does.

I remember another time, I was nervously going through prophecies about Jesus from the Old Testament, trying to get rid of some nagging doubts. As I was reading commentaries on these prophecies, I came across some from the Christian viewpoint and some from the Jewish viewpoint. This was not helping; it was making matters worse! Suddenly, in the middle of my frantic reading through the different views of who Jesus really is, these words came to me from my spirit. Though I had read comparable words in the Bible before, it came with a special anointing of the Spirit and with revelation, and it really did something in me. The words that came to me were these: "unless you have the faith of a little child."[38] There was no condemnation when these words came

---

[37] Romans 1:17 KJV.
[38] See Matthew 18:3; Mark 10:15; Luke 18:17.

to me, but they brought life in an otherwise very distressful situation. This is when I realized that there will always be those who do not recognize Jesus for who He really is and that I can't let that fact keep me in a place of double-mindedness. Trying to make sense of it all by hoping that everybody else agrees with me on what I believe would never be possible. But simple, childlike faith was to be my solution.

Out of this experience, I concluded that for a child of God the solution never is to look at other religions in order to prove to ourselves that they are indeed faulty nor is it to look at the opinions of others or at other belief systems. Trying to find peace by considering different viewpoints could never be the way of resolving any doubt issues. Though supernatural touches from God are extremely helpful to our faith and are part of our inheritance as believers in Jesus Christ, on the long run, a simple decision to believe the Word of God, which is empowered by God's grace and His Holy Spirit within, will keep our faith alive. And right there and then, I realized that just as I had begun this journey with simple, childlike faith, it was going to be that simple, childlike faith that was going to carry me through to the finish line.

This one statement spoken to me from the Holy Spirit in the right timing totally set me free. What ultimately brought peace to my analytical mind was the realization that when it's all said and done, unless we have the faith of a little child, we will in no wise enter into the kingdom of heaven.[39] It is so simple that many miss it!

Some people are too quick to give up. When you pray for God to help you, you can expect Him to do it. Give Him

_____

[39] See Matthew 18:3.

some time to come through for you. He is faithful to do it. You will be amazed that after some time has passed, you have already begun to change in that area and your faith has already grown. Again, I know now that if I experience doubt in any area, I simply need to go from faith to faith until I reach the level of conviction, the place where I have no more doubts, knowing all the while that God is patient and that He will help me.

You may also doubt the love God has for you. Jesus openly declared that His Father loved Him.[40] John frequently stated that he was the disciple whom Jesus loved.[41] I believe we need to learn from Jesus and John. Remember that night when God showed me what my problem was? I had two dreams which led to the same diagnosis: legalism. In the end of the second dream, I saw the heavenly Father; He had a folded, homemade card in His hands. I could see some writing in the card and there also was the contour of a little hand drawn in the card. I recognized it as a card that I had given Him out of great love for Him. The Father was looking at the card, weeping because His daughter was gone. When I saw Him weeping, my first response was, *He loves me?*

The Bible says in Romans 8:15, "For [the Spirit which] you have now received [is] not a spirit of slavery to put you once more in bondage to fear, but you have received the Spirit of adoption [the Spirit producing sonship] in [the bliss of] which we cry, Abba (Father)!" Father! If you have been having a hard time receiving the Father's love, it is imperative that you study the love of God until it becomes a reality in your life. And not only do you need to have an idea of the

---

[40] See John 3:35; John 5:20.
[41] See John 13:23; John 19:26; John 20:2; John 21:7; John 21:20.

general love of God, but you need to believe in His personal and intimate love for you. First John 4:16 says, "And we know (understand, recognize, are conscious of, by observation and by experience) and believe (adhere to and put faith in and rely on) the love God cherishes for us." This Scripture taken from the *Amplified Bible, Classic Edition* indicates that we receive the love of God for ourselves through faith and experience: "and believe the love God cherishes for us." Allow yourself to believe that God loves you personally. Meditate on the significance that you are the pupil of God's eye.[42] How sensitive God is to your hurt and pain! Open your heart afresh to Psalm 103:11, which says that as the heavens are high above the earth, so great are His mercy and loving-kindness toward those who reverently and worshipfully fear Him. God is love, and he who dwells and continues in love dwells and continues in God, and God dwells and continues in him.[43] Read Psalm 103:11, Zechariah 2:8, and 1 John 4:16 as though it were the very first time you read them. Romans 8:28–39 and Ephesians 3:16–21 are also very good Scriptures to study. Open your heart to them and allow yourself to believe them concerning you personally.

You can choose what you will believe. I love how Joyce Meyer puts it; she says, "Be a prisoner of hope."[44] We can believe the best, because in this case, the best is true, which is that God loves you indeed. He loves *you* very much, so much that He sacrificed His only Son for you so that you would be gratuitously reconciled with Him in love and you could enjoy a sweet fellowship and communion with your God.

---

[42] See Zechariah 2:8 AMPC.
[43] See 1 John 4:16.
[44] See also Zechariah 9:12.

Notice, in my dream I was still His daughter. That status or reference between me and Him hadn't changed; what had changed was that I had gone away from Him. I was still in His house physically, but my heart was far from Him.

Practically speaking, it is important to nurture our faith by going where faith is. Go to a Bible-believing church. Ask the Lord to send strong believers your way who have a solid faith walk with God. Read the Word. The less we read the Word of God, the more susceptible we will be to attacks of doubt. Again, the Word says that faith comes by hearing and hearing by the Word of God. Therefore, we need our regular intake of the Word of God to keep us strong and healthy in the faith.

I have also noticed that my faith works at its best when I know I pray according to God's will.[45] Then it is easy for me to expect God to step in and answer my prayers. Faith is going somewhere. Faith is active, it is not passive. Faith is filled with vision for the future. Faith expects to have what it believes, so it makes decisions accordingly.

People with living faith live their lives in harmony with what they believe will be the fulfilment of their prayers. They believe that as they seek God diligently and wholeheartedly, God will answer their prayers and will give them what they need to take the next step and then the next step and then the next step.[46] They see their future according to their prayer lives and live in accordance with what they expect God will do when they pray God's will. The Word of God is our road map. When we know the will of God for our lives and we co-

---

[45] See 1 John 5:14–15.
[46] See Hebrews 11:6.

operate with Him by taking steps of obedience by faith, we know that God will answer our prayers.

There is yet another facet of faith that I want to address before we move on to the next part of this chapter. While learning more and more to lean on God, I discovered that faith is made possible through humility. When we know we can't do it and we are helpless in the situation we are in, it places us in the perfect position to give up all attempts at helping ourselves and instead turn to God and depend entirely on Him to help us. We really need to learn to live in that place of surrender, where we give up trying in our own strength to make things happen and where we actively depend on God to help us, to guide us, and to give us the grace that we need to do what He wants us to do and to be who He wants us to be. Furthermore, it is a place where we give up trying to impress man, where we humbly pray to our invisible God and depend on Him to come through for us.[47] It is a place where we position ourselves to be prey to mockery, a place where, like Meshach, Shadrach, and Abednego, we can declare: "Whether He delivers me or not, I will not bow."[48] Andrew Murray explains it beautifully in His book *Humility*.

> We shall learn that faith and humility are at root one, and that we never can have more of true faith than we have of true humility; we shall see that we may indeed have strong intellectual conviction and assurance of the truth while pride is kept in the heart, but that it makes the living faith, which has power with God, an im-

---

[47] See John 5:44.
[48] See Daniel 3:16–18.

possibility. We need only think for a moment what faith is. Is it not the confession of nothingness and helplessness, the surrender and the waiting to let God work? Is it not in itself the most humbling thing there can be, the acceptance of our place as dependents, who can claim or get or do nothing but what grace bestows?! Humility is simply the disposition which prepares the soul for living on trust. And every, even the most secret breathing of pride, in self-seeking, self-will, self-confidence, or self-exaltation, is just the strengthening of that self which cannot enter the kingdom, or possess the things of the kingdom, because it refuses to allow God to be what He is and must be there—the All in All.[49]

It takes humility to receive the gift of salvation and to walk by faith. Jesus said that apart from Him we can do nothing, and He means what He says.[50] As long as we think that we can do it ourselves, it will be very hard to lean on God to do it. Pride causes us to try to earn our salvation so that we can boast of our accomplishment. However, the Bible is clear that "by grace are ye saved through faith; and that not of yourselves: it is the gift of God: Not of works, lest any man should boast."[51] That way, God eliminated pride.

We have learned in this section that doubt and unbelief are roots from which legalism grows. If you doubt what the

[49] Andrew Murray, *Humility* (New York: Anson D. F. Randolph & Co., 1895), http://www.worldinvisible.com/library/murray/5f00.0565/5f00.0565.09.htm.
[50] See John 15:5.
[51] Ephesians 2:8–10 KJV.

Bible says about who Jesus is, about His nature and about His love for you, or if you doubt what the Bible says about you, about who you are in Christ and about how God sees you, then you will be inclined sooner or later to take the matter into your own hands. This is exactly what legalism is, taking the matter into your own hands, which leads me to the next section.

> For the Lord takes pleasure in His people; He will beautify the humble with salvation and adorn the wretched with victory.
>
> —Psalm 149:4

Pride

> Look at the proud; his soul is not straight or right within him, but the [rigidly] just and the [uncompromisingly] righteous man shall live by his faith and in his faithfulness.
>
> —Habakkuk 2:4

About five years after I was born again, I had a dream. In the dream, I was a student, and I was sitting down at my desk in a classroom. There were other students with me, all Christians. Some of them were Christians whom I know in real life. The teacher was the evangelist Jesse Duplantis. It was time for our evaluation of how well (or how poorly) we had done to date. Jesse was standing in front of the class and he started pulling out our report cards, one by one. The first one was mine, and he said quite boldly: "Kathleen: pride; useless." He threw my file away and continued on. I was devastated! How could he just say something like that and not even care about how it made me feel? How could he discard me as useless and move on just like that? I walked out of the classroom heartbroken. The dream ended like that.

When I woke up, I thought, *Lord, pride? I just don't understand! What do you mean by pride? I mean, I don't think that I consider myself more highly than I ought to, do I? I sincerely don't think that I have a prideful attitude when I minister. I don't believe that I boast in myself. . . . I don't understand, Lord, what do you mean by pride?*

During those days we received monthly magazines from Jesse Duplantis Ministries, and we still do to this day. It may have been the very next day, but not more than a few days after the dream, that I picked up the monthly magazine and to my utter amazement saw that Jesse was scheduled to come to our hometown, Brampton, Ontario, within three weeks. I knew right then and there that God wanted to reveal to me the meaning of the dream through Jesse Duplantis himself.

When the time came, I went to Jesse's service and God did come through. The very first word that came out of Jesse's mouth was, "Pride." Wow, I was shocked! Even now I am still wondering if I really heard correctly. You can be sure that he had all my attention then. He referred to 1 Peter 5:6–7 KJV: "Humble yourselves therefore under the mighty hand of God, that he may exalt you in due time: Casting all your care upon him; for he careth for you." He went on to explain that when we do not cast our cares on God, it is due to pride. He also said that the greatest lesson that one could ever learn in life is to cast all of our cares on God.

This is when I learned that verse 7 cannot take place without verse 6. We need to humble ourselves if we ever want to be able to effectively cast our cares on God, not in order to comply with a law that says, "Thou must not be proud," but because if we don't first humble ourselves, we will still think that we can solve our problems in our own strength, and we will try to do it independently of God. Oh, we may say that we give it to God, but in reality we are still carrying the burden, still trying to fix our problem, or at least partially. But if we come to the place where we know that we can't do it (we humble and demote ourselves), then and only then can we successfully surrender and give our load to God for Him to take care of it and make everything right. Only then will we be able to leave everything at the altar and enter into the rest of God in that area.

As I look back, the cares that I carried were mostly pertaining to my desire to be like Jesus while being painfully aware of my weaknesses, my faults, and my sins. I felt like I had to be better, and I tried so hard to be better. I had no joy as a result, and while I thought that trying hard to change myself was godly, God didn't think so. He was well able to deal with my weaknesses, but He definitely was not happy about me not giving them to Him. See! Legalism is so deceptive. The Devil makes you think that by trying hard to be godly you are pleasing to God; when in reality, your trying hard *in your own strength* is the very thing that displeases God!

Trying to become like God apart from God, reminds me to an extent of Adam and Eve when they succumbed to the Devil's temptation. See what the Devil said to Eve in order to make her distrust her God and eat the forbidden fruit: "For God knows that when you eat from it your eyes will be opened, and you will be like God, knowing good and evil. When the woman saw that the fruit of the tree was good for food and pleasing to the eye, and also desirable for gaining wisdom, she took some and ate it. She also gave some to her husband, who was with her, and he ate it."[52]

See how quick Adam and Eve were to distrust God and begin to take matters into their own hands to reach the likeness of God? See how they wanted to obtain knowledge and wisdom and be like God through disobedience? Their great sin was their lack of trust in God. God had said in Genesis 2:16–17, "You are free to eat from any tree in the garden; but you must not eat from the tree of the knowledge of good and evil, for when you eat from it you will certainly die."

However, they did not rely on God but instead believed the lie of the Devil, which portrayed God as a liar, as a selfish master who wanted to keep them from what was best for them. Where am I going with this? Well, when we try to change ourselves in our own strength, we are giving into a similar temptation that Adam and Eve did. Instead of relying on God to mold us and to shape us into His image, we bite into the Devil's lie and pridefully think that we can carry out the work ourselves, apart from God, through disobedience to the law of faith.[53] The result? We become anxious because when we place ourselves under the law, we are made conscious of sin—of good and evil, and we feel like we don't measure up or we realize that we can't stop sinning no matter how hard we try. The Bible says that God resists the proud but He gives grace to the humble.[54] See how God resisted Sa-

---

[52] Genesis 3:5–6 NIV.
[53] See Romans 3:26–28 KJV.
[54] See 1 Peter 5:5 NKJV.

tan as a result of his pride. Jesus said that He saw Satan falling like a lightning from heaven.[55] Therefore, the harder we try in our own strength to please God, the more that God will resist us. It is a sure strategy for failure. Why? Because this shows that we think of ourselves more highly than we ought to; we think that we can be like Him apart from His grace. Strong words, aren't they? Believe me, I had to partake of this truth myself. Works of the flesh appeal to human pride.

I learned from the dream the Lord gave me that night that until we learn to stop trying in our own strength and to actively lean on Him in childlike trust and confidence (faith) that He will perfect that which concerns us,[56] we become useless to God. Why is that? It is because in that place, we are not in a position of trust and pliability in the hands of God. When we are full of care, we are not free to serve God nor are we free to be led by the Spirit of God. In that place, we take things into our own hands, which in turn ties God's hands from being able to effectively work in our situation. Don't confuse the word *useless* with *worthless*, for we are so valuable in God's eyes that He sent His only begotten Son to die for us so that we may live for eternity with Him. And when we understand the value He places on us and simply have faith (trust) in Him, we become effective for His kingdom.

I am not talking about a passive and inactive faith. Faith is very active, as we have discussed in the previous portion of this chapter. And as we expect God to work a change in us, God will do so; He also will show us what to do. Then, by faith and by depending on His Holy Spirit to give us the grace that we need, we begin to do the thing that He shows us

---

[55] See Luke 10:18.
[56] See Psalm 138:8.

to do. We become empowered by His very Spirit, and we will be able to obey Him and be what He wants us to be. But if we try to be the way we think God wants us to be without relying on the finished work of the cross for that and without depending on and asking God to make us that person first, we are in for big trouble and, really, we are wasting our time. The way we are changed is from the inside out, so our very hearts are changed. Our thoughts and our belief systems are transformed and renewed. We begin to share His thoughts and His purposes. We begin to have His heart manifested in our lives, and that's the way that our behaviors are changed, from the inside out. As we study the Word in the area of need and feed upon that Word, it renews us in the spirit of our mind.[57] And as we cooperate with the Lord, we begin to do the deeds we wanted to do; we begin to do them out of a heart of love and no longer because we are working to clear our guilty conscience, which is, by the way, very selfish.

Can you see it? We need the revelation that there dwells no good thing in the flesh and that no flesh will glory in His presence.[58] All of our righteousness is as filthy rags.[59] Instead, He gives us His righteousness as a free gift so we do not have to work for it.[60] As long as we work, God can't work. However, when we stop working, then God starts working. Where we end, God begins. Consequently, we will only be able to cast our cares on God when we come to the end of ourselves. Now let me ask you this, who do you think can do

---

[57] See Ephesians 4:23.
[58] See Romans 7:18; 1 Corinthians 1:29 KJV.
[59] See Isaiah 64:6.
[60] See Romans 5:17.

the best job, you or God? Yes, I am sure you figured it out; it is God. Therefore, waste no more time and believe.

The best care for self is to entrust ourselves to God who promises to take care of us and get busy doing good.[61] If we give ourselves to God, He will take way better care of us anyway than if we, in all our might, try to take care of ourselves. In fact, unless we give ourselves to God, He is not free to take care of us to the fullest. Only when we humble ourselves and give ourselves to God is He released to take care of us. That way, fear has no entrance. We become free from self, free to love, and free to serve God and others while God is taking care of us.

As already mentioned, the Bible says that God gives grace to the humble but He resists the proud. When we try to overcome our sin by ourselves, we can rest assured that we will fail at every turn. Not only are we unable to deliver ourselves, but God will see to it that every attempt fails; He will resist us and He will frustrate every effort at improving ourselves. Self cannot improve self. Instead, the only proper place for self is on the altar of the cross.[62] The Bible says that when Christ died, the old us died with Him.[63] Jesus said that apart from Him we can do nothing, and that means that apart from Him we can do nothing.[64]

You may say, well, I see it now, but it is so hard for me to stop trying in my own strength and to cast my cares on Him; I can't seem to be able to do it. The good news is that Christ died so that you could be free from pride, and if you

---

[61] See Psalm 37:3.
[62] See Romans 6:8.
[63] See Romans 6:6.
[64] See John 15:5.

will come to Him and ask Him to deliver you, He will. Why? Because two thousand years ago, He cried out, "It is finished." That means that He already said yes! But you cannot stop trying by trying to stop. You need to give it to God and ask Him to deliver you.

Again, the Bible mentions that salvation is free and no man can earn it. Subsequently, no one will be able to boast on that glorious day because they performed some good and honorable works or they made it due to their ability to obey God. We cannot even boast over our great faith! Instead, we depend on Him to provide the faith that we need. Therefore, just like the apostle Paul, let our declaration be: "But by the grace of God I am what I am."[65]

Pride wants to earn salvation. If one cannot work at earning his or her salvation, there remains no ground for boasting.[66] So pride will be a major obstacle to keep you from placing your faith in the finished work of the cross, because again, there is no room for boasting there. This is why in Isaiah 61 we read that God came to proclaim the good news to the meek.[67] If you lack humility, ask God to help you humble yourself, and He will help you freely.

It takes godly humility to cast our cares on Him, but it is pride to think that we can walk the Christian walk in our own strength and by our own self-effort. This indicates an independent spirit, a lack of faith, and a desire to stay in control of our lives. However, we have learned that this cannot be so in the life of the believer, for one must become entirely de-

---

[65] 1 Corinthians 15:10 KJV.
[66] See Romans 3:27.
[67] See Isaiah 61:1.

pendent upon the Lord or it is impossible for one to live at peace.

Learning to cast our cares on God is a journey and it takes time, but I can testify to what Jesse Duplantis said that night that learning to cast our cares on God is one of the greatest lessons one can learn in this life.

CHAPTER 4
COMING OUT OF LEGALISM

He called a little child to him, and placed the child among them. And he said: "Truly I tell you, unless you change and become like little children, you will never enter the kingdom of heaven. Therefore, whoever takes the lowly position of this child is the greatest in the kingdom of heaven.

—Matthew 18:2–4 NIV

Shortly after God revealed to me that legalism was my problem, I fervently asked the Lord, "What must I do that if I keep doing it, and doing it, and doing it, I will get better and better and better?" That night, glory be to God, I was able to fall asleep. It was 5:30 in the morning when an audible voice woke me up saying, "What must one do to go to heaven?" The voice began as a man's voice and quickly transformed into a child's voice. The child's voice sounded a lot like my son Aaron's, so I scanned the bedroom to see if he had come in. No one was there. Aaron would have been about six years old and he had already received Christ as his personal Lord and Savior. I remember that all Aaron knew then was that if he had Jesus, he was going to heaven. That's all he knew. He had Jesus, so he was saved, period. That morning, God showed me a foundational truth. He showed me that the faith and disposition of a healthy Christian is that of a child: innocent, trusting, carefree.

From that day on, I entered into a journey to learn how to become like a little child again. Someone who is innocent is free from condemnation, and someone who is trusting is free from care; he always expects to be accepted by his father regardless of his performance. A child does not complicate things; a child does not reason things out. A child is very simple. A child is free to enjoy himself. Furthermore, a child is not self-conscious, which means he doesn't spend his time focusing on himself, his failures, and his shortcomings. The child's responsibility is to obey his parents as they keep watch over him. If he doesn't obey, he is chastised; if he does well, he is praised. But a child never fears to be rejected by his parents; it's as simple as that.

I remember an incident at the beginning of my Christianity, before I fell into legalism. I fasted and prayed to get my way. Actually, I wanted Brian back. This was before I met Paul. I believe it was the second day of my fast when I felt the brief anger of the Father because I was insisting on getting something He already had showed me wasn't for me to have. Do you know what my response was? I was excited I had just had such a spiritual experience. I never felt condemned once. I never feared that He would reject me or that He would kick me out of heaven either. I knew, however, that I had tried my Father, and as a result, He did get angry for a moment. O but praise God His anger is only for a moment, and His favor is for a lifetime![1]

Just like a child is totally dependent on his parents for everything that concerns him, so we have to come to a place of complete dependency upon the Lord. Dependency on Him was probably the single most important key to my getting better. I wish I could tell you that I became like a little child the moment God showed me my way out of legalism was to

[1] See Psalm 30:5.

become like a little child again. But it took time and steps of faith to become like a little child again. I wanted to figure my way out. I was trying to stop being legalistic, but the more I tried, the more anxiety I felt. I knew by then that legalism was a terrible sin and that God hated everything about it, and yet I couldn't seem to stop the evil cycle. I remember one night in the midst of this, the Lord gave me a dream. In the dream, I was drowning, but I was desperately trying to save myself from drowning. Then, I saw on the shore a strong man, and I hoped that he could come and save me. God was showing me that I was powerless to save myself.

Finally, I called the prayer line of a ministry a pastor referred me to. During our conversation, the man on the other end of the line said to me these very wise words: "Remember that you won't come out the way you came in." Praise God for these inspired words! These words were so true and I knew that they were leading me closer to my deliverance. However, it took a long time before I could enjoy my Christian walk again.

The Bible says in Romans 5:6, "While we were yet in weakness [*powerless to help ourselves*], at the fitting time Christ died for (in behalf of) the ungodly)" (emphasis mine). This means we can't save ourselves and that every attempt will fail. As discussed in the previous chapters, God won't accept any fleshly effort on our part to save ourselves. All of our efforts are in vain. God will only accept the shed blood of the Lamb, Jesus Christ, as the payment for our sins; and nothing else will be received in His sight. The Bible is clear that it is the anointing that breaks the yoke and that it is not by might, nor by power, but by the Spirit of God.[2]

As I learned to depend on Him and to do what Isaiah 40:31, Isaiah 26:3, and Psalm 62:1 say, the Lord really began to work on my behalf.

> But they that wait upon the LORD shall renew their strength; they shall mount up with wings as eagles; they shall run, and not be weary; and they shall walk, and not faint.
>
> —Isaiah 40:31 KJV

> You will guard him and keep him in perfect and constant peace whose mind [both its inclination and its character] is stayed on You, because he commits himself to You, leans on You, and hopes confidently in You.
>
> —Isaiah 26:3

> For God alone my soul waits in silence; from Him comes my salvation.
>
> —Psalm 62:1

As a healthy born-again child of God, as long as our innocence is protected we will inherently *want* to obey God and we will naturally submit to God with gladness. However, as soon as we are told "thou must not sin" without a proper understanding of what Christ did for us at the cross, sin becomes alive and we die.[3] As long as we are innocent, that is, as

---

[2] See Isaiah 10:27 KJV; Zechariah 4:6.
[3] See Romans 7:9.

long as we live free from condemnation, we serve God because we love Him. As soon as we are told that we *must* not
sin, it renders us powerless to live victoriously and sin starts
to prevail in our lives; it defeats us. Why? Because as discussed in chapter 2, the law is the strength of sin.[4] I love what
I've heard Joyce Meyer say: "If we will stop reading the Word
because we *have* to, we will realize that we *want* to." And this
applies to everything that pertains to our Christian walk.

If you have been hiding from God in fear, don't. Don't
run from Him; run to Him! Condemnation wants us to hide
from God, and it sinks us deeper into sin because it declares
us guilty; it declares us sinners. We cannot rise above what we
believe to be God's verdict concerning us. If He declares us
sinners, no amount of works will make us righteous. However, if He declares us righteous, then life is good. And we know
from the Word that God pronounces as righteous those who
have placed their faith in Christ. Therefore, in spite of the
strong feelings of condemnation that you may be experiencing even now, it is important by faith to go against their insisting demands. It is important to run to God regardless of how
intense your feelings of guilt and condemnation may be. Even
if everything in you screams, "Sinner!" "Guilty!" "Hide from
God!" come to Him. In the midst of the torment, draw near to
Him. Even if everything in you says, "You are not acceptable
to God," come close to Him and ask Him to deliver you, and
He will. Come to Him with the innocence of a child, for to
such is the kingdom of heaven.[5]

When I went to the CEGEP, I had an inner "law" or
conviction whereby I just couldn't imagine having a score

---

[4] See 1 Corinthians 15:56 KJV.
[5] See Matthew 19:14.

lower than 80%. All I aimed for was 80% or higher. I wasn't a perfectionist, because I didn't even aim for 90%. I was satisfied with an 80% average. The passing mark, I believe, was 60%. But the passing mark was never in the realm of consciousness for me, because I aimed so much higher that I didn't fear failing the course; it didn't even cross my mind. My point is this, we need no longer focus on the salvation mark, on the "passing" mark, but we are free to focus our attention on higher levels where our goal can now be to know Him more, to enjoy Him more, to be more like Jesus, to grow in love, to fulfill the call of God for our lives, and to do the will of God. We have been freed to such an extent that our goal can be the perfecting of holiness and to hear His voice daily so that we can follow Him daily. The place of not making it to heaven (the 60% mark) is not a concern to us, because we know that it has already been taken care of by Christ at the cross for us who believe.

Deliverance from Legalism

> The Lord is my Rock, my Fortress, and my Deliverer; my God, my keen and firm Strength in Whom I will trust and take refuge, my Shield, and the Horn of my salvation, my High Tower.
> —Psalm 18:2

It might have been a year and a half after that God revealed to me that I was bound by legalism, I went for prayer at the altar. I wasn't in my home church but in a church of one of our pastor friends. A guest speaker was there. As I stood at the altar, the man of God approached me. I lifted up my hands in the air, and to my amazement, I lifted them up with the insides of my wrists facing me, each wrist closely situated side by side as though chained to each other. I knew it depicted the condition of my spirit. This is what legalism does to born-again children of God; it chains our spirits so that we are no longer free. However, the Bible clearly states that it is for freedom that Christ has set us free.[6]

When we are bound by legalism, demonic influences are definitely involved. We've already discussed that the spirit of witchcraft is the power behind legalism. I noticed through my experience that the spirit of legalism and the spirit of fear work together to ensnare us and they try to pull us back into legalism during the process of recovery.

Fear is the forceful spirit that attempts to draw us back into slavery every time if not resisted. Here is how I saw it work in my own experience. One night, I was at church and it was family night. Family nights happen once every quarter at our church, during which anyone can come up on the platform and edify the others with a testimony, a song, a poem, etc. I had been doing much better, and I did believe that I was either free or well on my way to complete freedom from legalism. However, legalistic thoughts (the spirit of legalism) began to harass me with jealousy followed by thoughts like, *You must not be jealous.* To which I would reply, *Oh no! I don't want to fall back into legalism! Oh, but I believe I felt some jealousy about so and so just now!* And so on and so forth. I became overly concerned and full of dread that legalism was going to find its way back in my life (spirit of fear). Instead of resisting jealousy in the power of the Spirit out of who I am in Christ (accepted, righteous, and free from jealousy); instead of resisting

---

[6] See Galatians 5:1 NIV.

legalism in faith, believing that I am forgiven of my sin and that I am not a legalist anymore through God; instead of leaning on Him to uphold me with His righteous right hand[7] while I was being attacked; I started to give in to fear more and more.

By this time, a lady was on the platform and she was sharing what a difficult situation she had found herself in with her daughter and how God helped her and kept her. She also coveted our prayers because she was still going through a hard time with her daughter. She then stepped down from the platform and came toward her seat, which was located in the row behind mine. When she reached her row and began to walk across the pews behind me, I felt I should touch her with a compassionate touch. When I touched her, I felt a kind of tingling sensation flow from my hand all through my arm and settled down on my heart. There it was again, the spirit of fear. It had found an open door and gained access that night because I failed to successfully resist in the faith the legalistic thoughts that bombarded my mind. I think I can safely say it took me at least two or maybe three months before I was freed from the spirit of fear again. This incident helped me better understand how the spirit of legalism and the spirit of fear work together to bind us or trip us up. It also showed me that it was very important for me to resist them in the faith.

It is important to fight from a standpoint of victory. "It is finished!" It's not because you feel victorious that you are victorious. The Devil will tempt us by making us feel jealous (for instance), and what he tries to do is to confuse feelings with our identity, with who or with what we are in Christ—

---

[7] See Isaiah 41:10 NIV.

righteous, free, and not jealous. What the Devil attempts to accomplish is to make us cave in to the pressure of temptation when it comes upon us in the form of feelings and thoughts. When that happens, we need to resist the temptation by faith, rebuking the Devil and quoting Scripture in the area under attack. We are called to fight the good fight of faith.

The Lord will lead you personally as to what is needed for your complete deliverance from legalism. The way the Lord chooses to deliver you may not be the exact same way He chose to bring deliverance in my life. However, one thing will always remain, and that is the truth. The truth of His Word will be the same, but the approach He uses to deliver you may differ from the one He used with me. Whether He delivers you on the spot, or whether God sees fit to take you through a process where deliverance comes little by little as you receive revelation of the truth from glory to glory, God is the one who must lead you *always*. He knows our makeup, and this is too delicate a procedure to involve man's ideas in the process. In all your ways acknowledge Him, and He promised that He will direct your steps and make your path straight.[8] Of course, God may use people as part of His deliverance kit to set you free and to teach you the truth or to guide you, but you must make sure to acknowledge Him first and to expect Him to lead you so when He does use people, you recognize that He is the one operating behind them or speaking through them.

Your deliverance will come purely on the basis of grace. There is nothing that you and I can do to earn deliver-

---

[8] See Proverbs 3:6.

ance. As children of God, we cannot work our way out of this mess. It *is* the anointing that *will* ultimately break the yoke.[9]

God is our deliverer and He promised to keep us if we will place our trust in Him. The Bible says that we do not fight against flesh and blood, but against principalities and powers in high places.[10] God promised to lead us when we acknowledge Him and make Him our source.[11] He will therefore show you what to do to be delivered from these demonic influences. Just come to Him and ask Him to show you what to do and expect Him to guide you. Tell Him that unless He delivers you, you won't be delivered. Acknowledge that apart from Him you can do nothing.[12] A broken and a contrite heart He will not despise.[13] And He will come speedily to your rescue. Simply humble yourself before Him, acknowledging your need of Him, and see Him work in your situation. You will have reason to praise Him once this whole ordeal is over, realizing that He is the one that will establish you and settle you in the faith.[14]

> Be well balanced (temperate, sober of mind), be vigilant and cautious at all times; for that enemy of yours, the devil, roams around like a lion roaring [in fierce hunger], seeking someone to seize upon and devour. Withstand him; be firm in faith [against his onset—rooted, established, strong, immovable, and determined], knowing

---

[9] See Isaiah 10:27 KJV.
[10] See Ephesians 6:12.
[11] See Proverb 3:6.
[12] See John 15:5.
[13] See Psalm 51:17.
[14] See 1 Peter 5:10.

that the same (identical) sufferings are appointed to your brotherhood (the whole body of
Christians) throughout the world. And after you
have suffered a little while, the God of all grace
[Who imparts all blessing and favor], Who has
called you to His [own] eternal glory in Christ
Jesus, will Himself complete and make you
what you ought to be, establish and ground you
securely, and strengthen, and settle you. To Him
be the dominion (power, authority, rule) forever
and ever. Amen (so be it).

—1 Peter 5:8–11

The Only Voice That Makes the Difference

The sheep that are My own hear and are listening to My voice; and I know them, and they follow Me.

—John 10:27

Through it all, I can safely testify that truly it is His
voice that made the difference. Each time I found myself falling again into the grip of legalism and cried out to Him, He
ultimately answered and provided me with a revelation that
brought me back on my feet. His voice led me to wholeness
again. Yes, we may have questions we feel need answers; but
we need to make sure that when we seek the answers by reading books, by asking people, or even when reading the Bible,
we always depend on the Lord and first ask Him to provide
us with the answers we feel we need and then expect Him to
provide them. Otherwise, we are setting ourselves up for defeat and for waves of diverging doctrines and opinions to

come our way without clear direction. If your desire is for your faith to be genuine and to increase, to be settled in the faith, make sure that in everything Christ is the source of your help.[15] Then the Lord may decide to speak to you through a book, a person, circumstances, His Word, directly to you, or in whichever way He chooses. The Bible says that He is an ever present help in times of trouble.[16] Do not settle for any other help than Christ's, and then let Him choose which way He will teach you.

While it appeared to me that the grace of God seemed so natural for many other Christians to understand and to abide in, for me it was extremely difficult to get it and to surrender to it. It really makes me think of how I learned to sing. It was the same thing for me, and God really taught me spiritual lessons during my singing lessons. For one, it seemed that so many people had a basic, innate understanding of how to sing and how to sing from the diaphragm. For me, it was so hard to understand how to make it work and, the thing is, no one could just jump inside my body and sing through me so that I could get it. Just the basic techniques of singing were so hard to make happen and to make work in me. By trial and error, I had to keep trying until I finally got it; and believe me when I say that it took many hours and a lot of hard work to get there. It took me nearly my entire three years of singing lessons to finally be able to project my voice on a more consistent basis and thus understand how to use my instrument (my body) for singing. It seemed to me that even people who didn't have singing lessons were better than I was for the longest time.

---

[15] See Colossians 1:23.
[16] See Psalm 46:1.

Coming Out of Legalism

It was the same when it came to understanding the whole "being saved by grace through faith" message. It was like a veil was over my understanding, and I just couldn't seem to be able to get it.[17] I would think, *You are saved by grace but you better not sin! Well, but I do sin every day it seems, so what does that mean?* Blah-blah-blah. . . . It almost drove me insane! And while others seemed to just enjoy their righteousness in Christ, I was insecure and so afraid of losing my salvation. I didn't understand how each piece of the puzzle was supposed to work together and even less how they could work in *harmony* with one another. As a result, I became extremely anxious, fearing hell every day; and I felt like I couldn't have peace until I could put all the pieces of the puzzle together.

Some people believed we are saved by grace through faith, while some believed in predestination. Others believed that we needed to work for our salvation. Others were mixing everything together, saying we are saved by grace through faith, but we better not sin! Still others said once saved, always saved. This whole confusion caused me to become obsessed with doctrines. I was afraid that if I chose the wrong doctrine, if my beliefs were erroneous, it would put me at risk of going to hell too; so I'd better find the exact answer or I'd be in trouble. But the problem was everybody I asked had a slightly different nuance of the doctrine of salvation. If there was one truth and if it was supposed to be so easy and so simple to get, then why was everybody teaching something different on what one would think is the foundation of Christianity?

---

[17] See 2 Corinthians 3:14–16.

It cost me many sleepless nights as I frantically wrote Scriptures upon Scriptures on pieces of paper in hopes of finding the answers to my questions and the resulting peace of mind. While in that condition, I had a hard time coming to the revelation knowledge of the truth. I was endlessly going in circles, tormented and in fear, going from Scripture to Scripture trying to find what the truth really was. I had a hard time committing to any of the beliefs on this for fear that I would pick the wrong one and end up in hell in the end. This brought a lot of double-mindedness in my life during that period. O what a pitiful mess I was!

Then one day, in His mercy, the Lord led me to a book that was sitting on our bookshelf, which I had never picked up to read before. This wasn't the kind of book I would normally be attracted to, and nothing on the cover or in the title appealed to me. However, that day, I felt the prompting of Holy Spirit to pick up that book. I did feel like I was on my way to recovery from legalism, which I was, but I wasn't completely free. There was yet another aspect of legalism which was haunting me because it had not been exposed yet. I hadn't recognized it as legalism. But I knew that whatever was still causing torment in my life was potentially legalism. I was praying to God to show me if I was indeed still dealing with legalism somehow, and I was asking Him to set me free from every trace, shape, and form of it. O and praise be to God, He revealed it to me that day and the truth set me free.

As I opened the book and scanned through the table of contents, one chapter caught my attention, and I went right to it. There it was, the answer to my dilemma. "If we are saved by doctrine then, for heaven's sake let's study! We don't need God, we need a lexicon. Weigh the issues. Explore the options. Decipher the truth. But be careful, student. For if you are saved by having exact doctrine, then one mistake would be fatal."[18] There it was, as I call it, the legalism of doctrine. The Lord provided the way to remove all confusion in the next chapter. "How do you simplify your faith? How do you get rid of the clutter? How do you discover a joy worth waking up to? Simple. Get rid of the middleman."[19] This was to be my solution, to get rid of the middleman and to tune in with God Himself. When it's all said and done, His voice is the only voice that will make a real difference in our lives.

Again, God will use people to help us, and the Bible says in Proverbs 11:14 that where no wise guidance is, the people fall, but that in the multitude of counselors there is safety. However, before we go to anyone for counsel, we need to go to *the* Counselor. The Bible tells us in John 14:26 that the Comforter (Counselor, Helper, Intercessor, Advocate, Strengthener, Standby), the Holy Spirit, whom the Father sent in Jesus' name, teaches us all things. And He causes us to recall everything that Jesus has told us. So God will teach each and every one of us individually if we will trust Him for it. This is part of our inheritance as believers in Jesus Christ: to hear His voice and to receive guidance from Him. Really, my breakthrough came from hearing God's voice. It came as I received revelation of the truth upon revelation of the truth upon revelation of the truth.[20] Jesus said that it is the truth that will make us free.[21] So if receiving revelation from God is our

---

[18] Max Lucado, *And the Angels Were Silent: The Final Week of Jesus* (Sisters, Oregon: Multnomah Publishers, Inc, 1992), 106.
[19] Lucado, *And the Angels Were Silent*, 114.
[20] See Colossians 3:10.
[21] See John 8:32.

answer, then how can we receive these revelations? This vital question leads me to the next part of this chapter.

Receiving Revelation through Prayer

The Lord is near to all who call on him, to all who call on him in truth.
—Psalm 145:18 ESV

As I look back and see where I came from and where I am now, I can tell you that prevailing prayer was key to my deliverance. As I acknowledged Him and sought Him with my whole heart throughout the entire recovery process, He came through every time. I remember standing in the washroom one day and proclaiming: "I declare before heaven and earth that unless Christ delivers me, I will not be delivered!" That day I made it clear to God and to the Devil that Christ would deliver me or I would perish, but no one or nothing else was going to do it for me. I had given my life to the gospel message, either it was true or it wasn't, but I would give it my all and completely jump at the risk of dying, because I had come that far. Sink or swim, I knew that Christ was alive and now was the time to really prove Him.

There is certainly something that releases God's power when we reach the end of ourselves and make Jesus the only option. Again, the Bible says that He is a very present help in times of trouble, and I can testify of that in my own life.[22] He promises that those who ask will receive, those who seek will find, and to those who knock, the door will be opened.[23] He

---

[22] See Psalm 46:1.
[23] See Matthew 7:7–8.

also said in His Word that if we will seek Him with our whole heart, we will find Him.[24] The apostle Paul boldly declared in Ephesians 3:20 that God is able to do superabundantly, far over and above all that we dare pray, ask, think, or dream according to the power that is at work within us. The Bible further says that if we pray according to God's will, He hears us, and if we know that He hears us, we know that we have that which we asked of Him.[25] We can rest assured that complete deliverance from legalism is His will, so we can trust that He will do just as He promised and deliver us as we keep believing in Him to do it. Because of the finished work of the cross, the answer to our cry for deliverance is yes. Therefore, we need not worry whether God really wants to help us or not.

The revelation of the finished work of the cross revolutionized my prayer life and my faith walk. Now I know that no matter the stronghold, when I have a struggle, I go to the Father in Jesus' name (representing all that He is and all that He has done for us on the cross), and I know that His answer is yes because Jesus cried, "It is finished," two thousand years ago. Additionally, praying God's Word is powerful because His Word describes His very will for our lives and His promises to us.

Another very important piece of information concerning your prayer life: when you pray, do not keep all of your options open, but trust God. I love how it is translated in The Message version of the Bible: "If you don't know what you're doing, pray to the Father. He loves to help. You'll get his help, and won't be condescended to when you ask for it. Ask boldly, believingly, without a second thought. People who 'worry

---

[24] See Jeremiah 29:13.
[25] See 1 John 5:15 NIV.

their prayers' are like wind-whipped waves. Don't think you're going to get anything from the Master that way, adrift at sea, keeping all your options open."[26]

I had realized I couldn't just wake up and say, oh, that struggle with legalism was only a dream, no! I was really experiencing it, and I really had to confront and defeat legalism in the power of God's might. I felt as though I was thrown into the deep and was told to swim or sink; it was going to be one or the other. I was paddling for dear life. This place I found myself in was not simply a virtual place as in a movie, but it was reality. I was not watching a life story; I was living the main character. And I was going to sink unless I started some serious praying! This is when I really learned to depend on the Lord and to wait on Him for my deliverance. Through this process of praying to the Lord and depending on the Lord, I was becoming like a little child again as the Lord was remolding me on the inside little by little.

Hence, a key element that got me out of this mess was *prevailing prayer*. Each time I prayed to God with my whole heart I knew that He heard me. In a nutshell, this is the way I got out of legalism, one prayer at a time, one cry at a time, one supplication at a time. As a result of my crying out to Him, He would speak to me and give me a revelation that would pull down one more lie of the Devil, then another lie of the Devil, then another lie. . . . I am so amazed that each time we cry out to God with our whole heart, God always hears and answers. Truly, the Lord is nigh unto them that are of a broken heart and saves such as be of a contrite spirit.[27]

---

[26] James 1:6 MSG.
[27] See Psalm 34:18 KJV.

If you feel especially low in faith and in strength and if you are tired after a long day of work, ask the Holy Spirit to help you pray and He always will. Then, by faith alone, start praying, believing that the Holy Ghost is helping you, empowering you. Believe that He is giving you the faith that you need and the brokenness of heart that you need, and begin to pour out your heart to God. Then—and if there is one thing that you need to remember from this chapter, it is this—once you have prayed to God, you must actively expect Him to answer; you must actively expect Him to speak, and you must be actively listening. Doing that is living by faith. Because you believe that you have that which you asked of Him in prayer (in this case revelation knowledge, the truth needed to make you free), it follows that you will expect to receive it from God as a result of your prayer; and God will always come through for you; this is a promise from His Word. [28]

I also know how guilt and condemnation are very strong temptations when you are deep in legalism. However, I urge you not to shrink from God due to heavy condemnation. Instead, come to Him and pray anyway. God is for you, He is not against you.[29] He knows that you are under heavy loads of guilt and condemnation due to the deception that comes with legalism, and He is the only one who can rescue you from that demonic oppression. Remember that condemnation is not from God, but it is from the Devil; for he is the one who accuses the brethren before the throne of God day and night.[30] I will ask you to go against your feelings if you must, feelings of condemnation, shame, and guilt, and pray to

---

[28] See Mark 11:24.
[29] See Romans 8:31.
[30] See Revelation 12:10.

your God who is bigger and more than able to see you through. ·

When you pray, ask to know the root cause of your problem. The main theme of my prayer life during my recovery process was, "What is wrong with me?" That is what I prayed to God in faith over and over again, and God was faithful to give me the answer I was looking for seemingly every time. Once you know the root cause, ask Him to remove it and replace it with Himself and with His truth, and trust Him to do it and ask Him to show you your part. Stand on His promise that He will direct you and make your path straight as you acknowledge Him.[31] I prayed Proverbs 3:6 so many times throughout my own journey.

Finally, ask Him for the grace to do what He shows you to do. Again, make sure to stand on the Word of God to support your request. For instance, the following Scripture helped me a lot as I sought to follow God's counsel: "For it is God who works in you both to will and to do for His good pleasure."[32]

Don't get discouraged if at times you don't feel anything when you pray. All it takes to be heard is faith. When you pray, believe that you have received, and you will have that which you asked of Him.[33]

Prevailing prayer along with standing on the Word of God have been central parts of my recovery, and without them, I would not have made it.

---

[31] See Proverbs 3:6.
[32] Philippians 2:13 NKJV.
[33] See Mark 11:24.

Overcoming by the Word

You are my hiding place and my shield; I hope in Your word.

—Psalm 119:114

Maybe two years had passed since God had showed me I needed to become like a little child again and I was beginning to do much better. I had definitely not arrived yet, but at least I had some periods of time when I experienced more peace. However, I could sense that legalism was at arm's length, and I was starting to feel a little anxiety trying to creep in again. The Lord, in His mercy, saw what was going on and gave me a dream one night. In the dream, I was in an adulterous affair (again) and people were hurt as a result (remember in the second chapter of this book where I made mention that legalism is spiritual adultery?). At some point in the dream, I came to my senses and realized what I was doing and said something like this: "I don't want to continue doing this. I want to stop this!" After I said these words, I saw myself sitting at a desk in some kind of an office room. I was reading the Bible, and I could see that I was studying it with much intensity because I wanted to break free from the power of that sin. Suddenly a strong impression which neared the sound of a voice said, "Remember that you cannot overcome in your own strength but by the Word of God." And the dream ended.

Before I had the dream, I had come to know that God's Word was important, but I didn't realize just how much. After God gave me this dream, I really began to place my trust in His Word as an act of faith and obedience. I realized that His

Word living and abiding in me was going to be a vital con-
tributor to my permanent victory and that without it, I
wouldn't be able to remain standing. The Bible says that His
truth is a shield and a buckler to us.[34] The Bible also tells us to
use our sword, the Word of God, in battle.[35] Therefore, as an
act of faith, I began placing my hope in His Word. Instead of
trying to figure things out, I trusted His Word to renew me
inside. I trusted His Word to fight my battles. When I felt
powerless, I relied on the Word that I meditated upon and the
Word that I spoke out of my mouth to do the job. More and
more I stopped trying in my own strength, and instead I let
the Word of God do what only the Word of God can do. My
work became to study the Word, to listen to the Word, to
meditate upon the Word, and to speak the Word. That was
my part which was done by faith. God and His Word would
do the rest.

Jesus said in John 8:31–32 that if we abide in His Word,
then are we His disciples indeed; and we shall know the truth,
and the truth shall make us free. It is knowing the truth of the
Word of God and applying it to our lives that will cause victory over sin, not our desperate effort not to sin or to stop legalistic inclinations.[36] The more we try to stop sinning, the more
sin is on our mind, and the more we are prone to go back to it.
Christ is offering us a better way. He is offering us forgiveness
of sin so that we no longer have to be obsessed with it and instead we can fix our eyes on Him who is the Author and the
Finisher of our faith.[37] As we do this, bondages will begin to

---

[34] See Psalm 91:4.
[35] See Ephesians 6:17.
[36] See James 1:22.
[37] See Hebrews 12:2 KJV.

fall away. As we keep our eyes on Him and trust Him to deliver us from sin, He will.[38] As we place our hope in His Word, the Word will fight for us as long as we believe it, confess it, and do it. This can take time, but the Bible promises that if we keep doing what is good, we will reap if we faint not.[39]

However, if we keep reminding ourselves that we have a stronghold in our lives and keep trying in our own strength to stop it, it will enslave us. The more we try to put an end to it, the more we will fail. Does that sound familiar? Instead, true repentance of the heart causes us to desire change, and the washing of the Word of God by which our minds get renewed day by day transforms from the inside out. James said that when we receive and welcome the Word in meekness, it has the power to save our souls.[40] The Word can save our minds. As we study the Word of God, our way of thinking and our very belief system are changed and brought into subjection to the knowledge of Christ and to the will of God. Romans 12:2 puts it this way: "Do not be conformed to this world (this age), [fashioned after and adapted to its external, superficial customs], but be transformed (changed) by the [entire] renewal of your mind [by its new ideals and its new attitude], so that you may prove [for yourselves] what is the good and acceptable and perfect will of God, even the thing which is good and acceptable and perfect [in His sight for you]."

The Word of God is our spiritual sword with which we pull down, destroy, and overthrow strongholds in our lives.

---

[38] See Matthew 1:21.
[39] See Galatians 6:9 KJV.
[40] See James 1:21 KJV.

Then, with the same Word, we build and plant.[41] The Word is trustworthy. We can place our hope in God's Word and see the results in our lives. We can bank on it. God spoke to my husband and I one day and said, "Invest in me." I love it! Sometimes it takes time before we start seeing the results of our investment in the Word, but if we will be patient, sooner or later it will bear the harvest.

I strongly encourage you to read Scriptures relating to your area of need. If you struggle with legalism, then find Scriptures that can help you overcome legalism and renew your mind with the truth. You need to find Bible verses that are relevant to your specific need. The internet is a very useful tool that can help you find Scriptures and search by topic. I also encourage you to ask the Lord to guide you to anointed Christian books on the topic at hand. I read many Christian books during my recovery process. The more I kept my mind busy with the Word, the less opportunity the Devil had to distract me with his lies, and I became stronger in the Lord. The Devil's lies began to be exposed, and I began to know the truth more and more. It became easier and easier to counteract the Devil's lies with the Word of God and to stand my ground in faith.[42]

It is very important for us to understand that we are not reading the Word in order to meet God's expectations. Through what Jesus did on the cross, we have been delivered from the law (trying to meet God's expectations) as a means of righteousness with God.[43] Instead, we are reading the Word because it is our daily bread and because we love it and we

---

[41] See Jeremiah 1:10.
[42] See 1 Peter 5:9.
[43] See Romans 10:4.

love God. If we read the Word out of duty, it will minister death to us; it will steal the life and the joy that should come from reading Scriptures.[44] It is important for us to understand that.

Our motivation is, and our way of thinking now is: I am reading the Word because I love the Word! I also read it to receive my sustenance; it is my spiritual food to stay strong and healthy. Just like I eat natural food every day to keep my natural body alive and strong and full of energy, I need my spiritual food, which is the Word of God.

Renewing Your Mind

For to us a Child is born, to us a Son is given; and the government shall be upon His shoulder, and His name shall be called *Wonderful Counselor*, Mighty God, Everlasting Father [of Eternity], Prince of Peace.

—Isaiah 9:6 (emphasis added)

The Lord is our Counselor. We can safely run to Him to counsel us back to a sound mind. I don't remember if it was only a few months before I cried out to the Lord in the car that day, asking Him to reveal to me what my problem was. It could have easily been longer than that, but God gave me a dream. In the dream, I saw myself and the assistant pastor of our church. Then, I saw my head . . . but really it was my mind that I was seeing, or the condition of my mind. The entire area was red, like with fire. This is when I said to the as-

---

[44] See 2 Corinthians 3:7.

sistant pastor, "Unless God saves me, I cannot be saved." And that was the dream.

Through that dream, God showed me that my entire mind was sick and that only He could save it. It was a very troubling dream. After all, just consider for a moment being told that your entire head is sick with not even one tiny spot of it being right. I certainly was a helpless case apart from Him. But that is exactly it, *apart from Him*. The Bible tells us that with Him all things are possible. I am adamant that complete deliverance is possible and no one can tell me otherwise. God promised to deliver us from *all* our fears, not only some of them.[45] The Bible tells us that we have not been given a spirit of fear but of power, and of love, and of a sound mind.[46] I have the conviction that as we trust Him, He will deliver us from all of our fears and from the Devil's schemes, because He promised it in His Word. I believe that we can be 100 percent set free from the grip of legalism. We need only to not give up but to keep trusting God and cooperating with the Holy Spirit during the entire process of deliverance. It does take active faith, determination, and patience. This is why the Bible says in Galatians 6:9, "And let us not lose heart and grow weary and faint in acting nobly and doing right, for in due time and at the appointed season we shall reap, if we do not loosen and relax our courage and faint."

I have been grieved to read online from well-meaning people things like, "You can never be completely set free from legalism," or, "This is the way that you are, full of fearful thoughts and tormenting fears, but, oh, how God is proud of you to bear under that day after day." *These are lies*. It angers

---

[45] See Psalm 34:4.
[46] See 2 Timothy 1:7 NKJV.

me when I read falsehoods like that. Either Jesus is Lord and His work at the cross is perfect and complete or He is not and we have no hope. But I have good news for you, Jesus is alive and well on planet Earth, and He will set completely free anyone who will place their trust in Him and not give up until they abide in the freedom that Christ died to give them.

In one of the dreams that the Lord gave me in the early years of my Christianity, I found myself in front of a big TV screen, and on the screen a big, evil monster appeared and tried to intimidate me with his roar. He came with everything he had. I love how I responded. I turned off the TV as I exclaimed, "Oh you!" This is the way it also goes with the thoughts that the Devil tries to harass us with. When the Devil comes to us with his forceful lies and fearful thoughts, we have to learn to turn off the channel, the Devil's frequency, where all of the devilish thoughts abide, and instead to change the channel to God's channel, God's frequency, where all of God's thoughts abide, and tune in with God there. This is why the apostle Paul in Philippians encourages us to dwell on thoughts that are true. "Finally, believers, whatever is true, whatever is honorable and worthy of respect, whatever is right and confirmed by God's word, whatever is pure and wholesome, whatever is lovely and brings peace, whatever is admirable and of good repute; if there is any excellence, if there is anything worthy of praise, think continually on these things [center your mind on them, and implant them in your heart]."[47]

In addition, confession is also very important to the renewing of our mind. The Bible tells us to call those things that

---

[47] Philippians 4:8 AMP.

be not as though they were.[48] Speaking the truth with our mouth from the heart in accordance with the Word of God, even if those truths are not a reality in our lives yet, is very powerful. The Bible says in Proverbs 18:21 that life and death reside in the power of the tongue, so what we say about ourselves has tremendous power over our lives whether for life or for death.

"Now faith is!" I said this statement many times during my recovery. Every day I expected a breakthrough of some sort. Every day I got up and expected God to bring deeper revelation that would contribute to the renewing of my mind and to more freedom. I can describe my journey toward wholeness as many mini-breakthroughs day after day, one after another, toward the completion of the entire puzzle.

During my fight for my freedom from legalism, it was very important for me to fill my mind with the truth and to meditate on the Word day and night.[49] I meditated on Scriptures purposely and every time I had the chance throughout the day. I was desperate, so I constantly mused over the Word in my mind or I confessed it out loud. I would also write Scriptures on a piece of paper over and over again just to help with making them sink in and with memorizing them. Again, because my understanding of the Word had been so darkened, I read many Christian books whenever I could that were related to freedom from legalism, the nature of God, the renewing of the mind, freedom from fear, and how to overcome doubts. This was very edifying for me. Reading these books protected my mind from being bombarded with any

---

[48] See Romans 4:17 KJV.
[49] See Psalm 1:2; Psalm 119:11.

unwanted thoughts, and it kept my mind busy thinking on what was lovely, good, pure, true, and worthy of reverence.

However, my fight for freedom was anything but easy. My period of recovery included many falls as I learned to walk; I would get up by God's direct intervention, then fall again, get up, fall, get up. . . . I had to do what Isaiah said: "For the Lord God helps me; therefore have I not been ashamed or confounded. Therefore have I set my face like a flint, and I know that I shall not be put to shame."[50] People tend to give up too quickly. When they fall a couple of times they think that there is no hope for them and they give up, not really understanding how it works. Yet the Bible says in Proverbs 24:16 that a righteous man falls seven times and gets back up again! It requires commitment and determination.

Why am I sharing all of this in this section of the book? It is because the renewing of the mind takes time. While the Lord is working a change in us, it is important to keep our hopes up by putting on the helmet of salvation, because the very nature of the helmet is hope.[51] We need to be very patient with ourselves, knowing that God is patient with us. Remember that legalism always involves wrong thinking and wrong beliefs. Those thinking patterns and strongholds may have been formed over a long period of time. God is well able to set us free on a dime and to literally press the delete button and fill our minds with the truth if that's the way He wants to go about it. Normally though, He takes us through a recovery process where our minds get renewed from one level of glory to the next level of glory by the Spirit of God and by the

---

[50] Isaiah 50:7.
[51] See 1 Thessalonians 5:8; Ephesians 6:17.

knowledge of His Word.[52] With God's help, we pull one stronghold down and replace it with the truth, then another stronghold, then another lie, and another deception. And we replace them with the truth, so that little by little our minds get renewed until one day we wake up and find ourselves praising God for His counsel because we can think straight again! God reassures us that, after we have suffered for a little while, He Himself will establish us firmly.[53] Regardless of your current condition, God is well able to deliver you, only trust Him to do it.

One other thing is important to mention. The Word of God states that unless the hearing of the Word of God is mixed with faith, it will profit us nothing.[54] So the renewing of the mind has a lot to do with our becoming convinced of the truth. Only as we begin to believe the Word that we read or that we hear are we really being transformed and set free. So to the degree that we believe the Word, to that same degree are we being set free. Therefore, the renewing of the mind is, in a way, the renewing of our belief system. And remember that faith comes by hearing and hearing by the Word of God. All of this is made possible by the intervention of the Holy Spirit as we trust Him to give us the revelation of His Word.

This process requires patience. If we believe that we must be perfect the moment we realize that we have a problem, it will defeat us on the spot. I myself fell prey to that pressure many times. For instance, when God showed me that I was under legalism, I felt pressured that I had to stop all of it right away, the moment I was made aware of my state. The

---

[52] See 2 Corinthians 3:18.
[53] See 1 Peter 5:10.
[54] See Hebrews 4:2 KJV.

problem was, even if I wanted to stop, and even if I tried hard to stop it all, I just wasn't able to stop the legalistic thoughts and feelings and urges. This caused me to enter into works of the flesh, trying hard in my own strength to come out of legalism. I was trying to come out the way that I came in. Thinking that we must be perfect or that we must have a perfectly renewed mind the moment God shows us that we have a problem is a hindrance, not a help. However, in order for me to get that, God had to teach me what repentance really is.

Understanding Repentance

> Bear fruits that are deserving and consistent with [your] repentance [that is, conduct worthy of a heart changed, a heart abhorring sin]. And do not begin to say to yourselves, We have Abraham as our father; for I tell you that God is able from these stones to raise up descendants for Abraham.
>
> —Luke 3:8

One day, as had been my custom during my period of recovery from legalism, I asked the Lord, "What is wrong with me? What is my problem?" Somehow, I had fallen right back into the snares of legalistic thinking, and I couldn't seem to find my way out nor did I understand why I had fallen *again*. In His mercies, God showed me in a dream that night what my problem was. In the dream, I saw the well-known evangelist Jesse Duplantis; he was ministering in a church that was located in a strip mall. After the service ended, I walked out of the church and, lo and behold, he was right there. I was so excited!

Without wasting any time, I asked him a question that went something like this: "If someone offended me, and I chose to forgive that person, but I still have bad feelings toward the person, however because I chose to forgive, I am actively working with God and cooperating with Him to see my feelings and my heart changed toward that person, am I okay?"

To which Jesse answered these life changing words: "Don't you understand repentance?" That was the dream.

You see, during those days, I was especially tormented with the Scriptures that tell us that unless we forgive our offenders, we will not be forgiven by our heavenly Father. Matthew 6:14–15 is one of them. There are other Scriptures teaching us this principle also. I knew from Scriptures that choosing to remain in unforgiveness was wrong and even dangerous. I was very concerned because sometimes when people offended me, I went through a period where my feelings didn't align right away with my decision to obey God and forgive them. I was very troubled with this, and I desperately wanted to understand this matter. What if I died when my feelings had not completely caught up with my decision to forgive?

Not understanding the basic concept of repentance was a humbling thing for me. I knew that the question the evangelist asked me in the dream was a fair question, and I perceived that legalism had obscured the true meaning of repentance in my life. Through that dream, God taught me that repentance was a matter of the heart. He showed me that what God is looking for is a change of heart regarding sin; it is the choice to obey Him and to turn from our sins. Fruit of such repentance then begins to flow out of the sincere decision to turn from our sins, and our feelings progressively catch up with our decision. This, according to the dream, was acceptable repentance to God. Just like the Amplified Bible declares in Luke 3:8, repentance is to have a changed heart. When our hearts are changed concerning sin, fruit for repentance will naturally follow. In the dream, I had chosen to forgive (I had repented), but my feelings had not caught up quite yet. However, I was actively working *with* God to see my feelings changed toward the person that offended me (fruit for repentance). Repentance is an attitude of the heart first, and the fruit or the manifestation of repentance will naturally follow.

According to the *Amplified Bible, Classic Edition*, repentance involves the change of one's mind for the better, heartily amending one's ways, with abhorrence of his past sins.[55] It is a place where we agree with God and His Word concerning sin. It means turning away from, walking in the opposite direction. When we have a change of mind, our natural response will be to turn from it, and, by depending on God's grace and applying God's Word, begin to walk in the opposite direction. Repentance consists of the change of one's attitude toward God and toward sin. When the evangelist asked me, "Don't you understand repentance?" he was basically saying, "Yes, of course you are right with God because you *chose* to forgive; you agreed with God concerning the need to forgive. You are simply in the process of walking it out with God."

---

[55] See Mark 1:4 AMPC; Luke 5:32 AMPC; Luke 15:7 AMPC.

I believe it was Finney that said, in essence, that wherever we find saving faith, we also find repentance and the love of God; wherever we find repentance, we also find saving faith and the love of God; and wherever we find the love of God, we also find saving faith and repentance. The following Scriptures illustrate this principle very well.

> To whom God would make known what is the riches of the glory of this mystery among the Gentiles; which is *Christ in you, the hope of glory*.
> —Colossians 1:27 KJV (emphasis added)

> Then will I sprinkle clean water upon you, and you shall be clean from all your uncleanness; and from all your idols will I cleanse you. *A new heart will I give you and a new spirit will I put within you*, and I will take away the stony heart out of your flesh and give you a heart of flesh. And *I will put my Spirit within you and cause you to walk in My statutes, and you shall heed My ordinances and do them*.
> —Ezekiel 36:25–27 (emphasis added)

> No one born (begotten) of God [deliberately, knowingly, and habitually] practices sin, for God's nature abides in him [His principle of life, the divine sperm, remains permanently within him]; and he cannot practice sinning because he is born (begotten) of God.
> —1 John 3:9

We know that we have passed over out of death into Life by the fact that we love the brethren (our fellow Christians). He who does not love abides (remains, is held and kept continually) in [spiritual] death.

—1 John 3:14

The foregoing Scriptures describe someone who is in Christ; that is, someone who has placed their faith in Christ for the salvation of their soul. The result? A new nature; one that cannot practice sinning and one that possesses the love of God.

I remember being tormented with the "system" of confession; I feared that if I didn't have time to confess one sin before I died, I would end up in hell as a result. Confessing my sins had become a law to me. After all, doesn't the Bible teach us that if we confess our sins, He is faithful and just to forgive our sins and to cleanse us from all unrighteousness?[56] These four Scriptures helped me understand that such fear was unreasonable and unscriptural. I began to realize that Christ in me was my hope of glory, and my hope was not my perfect performance or my carefully ensuring that not one sin went unnoticed. I began to see that I had a new heart and a new nature. (Remember we mentioned at the beginning of this section that repentance is first and foremost a changed heart?) Isn't it great news that we now have God's very nature? Isn't it wonderful news that we have freely been made right through the sacrifice of Christ on the altar of the cross so

---

[56] See 1 John 1:9.

we could freely receive through faith a new heart, a heart which abhors sin, a heart which has a repentant attitude?

Confession is a fruit of an already repented heart; someone who has been made right with God through Christ has a repentant heart and will therefore naturally confess their sin as a result. Such a one will be quick to confess their sin when they become aware that they have sinned for their desire is to walk holy before the Lord. I began to realize that righteousness is a condition of the heart just like sin is a condition of the heart. Well, with Christ in me, my heart condition has gloriously changed from death to life. Now, from glory to glory He is changing me and making me in His image until the day of Jesus Christ. All the while I am accepted in the beloved. I love how Joyce Meyer puts it in her book *God Is Not Mad at You*: "Please notice that the Holy Spirit does not only convict us of sin, but goes on to convince us of righteousness. We are in right standing with God through the blood of Jesus, and we must always remember that— especially when we sin. We don't lose our fellowship with God each time we make a mistake. He never leaves us or forsakes us, but He is with us always. The moment you are convicted of sin, turn to Jesus, because it is only His blood that saves us. . . . Sin is only a problem for us if we continue in it after having been shown the awfulness of it. If we willfully refuse to turn away from it, then it will consume us. God's grace meets us where we are, but it never leaves us where it found us."[57]

* * *

---

[57] Joyce Meyer, *God Is Not Mad at You: You Can Experience Real Love, Acceptance & Guilt-Free Living* (Great Britain: Hodder & Stoughton, 2013), 155.

She will bear a Son, and you shall call His name
Jesus [the Greek form of the Hebrew Joshua,
which means Savior], for He will save His people from their sins [that is, prevent them from
failing and missing the true end and scope of
life, which is God].

—Matthew 1:21

CHAPTER 5
THE FINISHED WORK OF THE CROSS

When Jesus had received the sour wine, He said,
It is finished! And He bowed His head and gave
up His spirit.

—John 19:30

You already have everything it takes. Jesus did every-thing that will ever be needed for you and me. Every victory finds its source at the cross. When Jesus cried, "It is finished," He had just accomplished all that would ever be needed in order to secure our victory no matter what we face. Before your problem even started, Jesus already won the victory. This is why I am convinced that God is always willing to set us free from sin, because He has perfected us already through His single offering of Himself on the cross.[1] He has given us everything that pertains to life and godliness through the knowledge of Him.[2] These words mean that victory over sin is assured. All we need to do is to trust Jesus and follow Him as He leads us out of darkness and into His marvelous light.[3] He already said yes two thousand years ago to anyone who believes.

I really want you to get this. When I understood the finished work of the cross, it gave me boldness in prayer and assurance that He would answer. A Scripture that illustrates this well is Joshua 1:3: "Every place upon which the sole of your foot shall tread, that have I given to you, as I promised Moses." On the same token, through the cross God has al-

---

[1] See Hebrews 10:14.
[2] See 2 Peter 1:3 NKJV.
[3] See 1 Peter 2:9.

ready provided everything that we will ever need to walk in victory. All we need to do now is to appropriate it. After all, doesn't the Bible say that heaven suffers violence and that the violent take it by force?[4] As you stand firm in your faith in Christ and what He has done for you, you can come boldly before the throne of grace in times of need, and you can rest assured that God will help you.[5] Therefore, it is time to rise in faith and to take what is rightfully ours through Christ: our blood-bought-and-paid-for inheritance, which consists of righteousness, peace, and joy in the Holy Ghost![6]

We are called to fight the good fight of faith, and this battle against legalism is exactly it. We may not have realized it, because, again, legalism is very deceptive. I said it before, we have not been called to try but to believe. This is the good fight of faith: that we overcome condemnation through our faith in Jesus Christ.

Now, believe it or not, until we let go and let God, sin *will* have dominion over us. However, here is the amazing thing, if we will stop trying and instead simply receive the grace of God freely, we will experience freedom from sin. How can I say that? Because of Romans 6:14 KJV: "For sin shall not have dominion over you: for ye are not under the law, but under grace." If you find yourself struggling again with an old sin and can't seem to have the power to stop, ask yourself if you have brought yourself back under the law in that area. So we are only really safe when we are under grace. This also marries very well with Titus 2:11–12: "For the grace of God (His unmerited favor and blessing) has come forward

---

[4] See Matthew 11:12 NKJV.
[5] See Hebrews 4:16.
[6] See Romans 14:17.

(appeared) for the deliverance from sin and the eternal salvation for all mankind. It has trained us to reject and renounce all ungodliness (irreligion) and worldly (passionate) desires, to live discreet (temperate, self-controlled), upright, devout (spiritually whole) lives in this present world." This Scripture tells us that grace actually teaches us to live godly lives. The more grace we abide in, the hungrier we become for righteousness. Hence, we see that our only hope of ever living in victory over sin is by surrendering to and receiving the grace of God. I think it was Spurgeon who said, "We were not saved *in* our sins or saved *for* our sins... but saved *from* our sins." [7] Jesus put it this way: "Very truly I tell you, everyone who sins is a slave to sin. Now a slave has no permanent place in the family, but a son belongs to it forever. So if the Son sets you free, you will be free indeed."[8]

Placing No Confidence in the Flesh

But whatever were gains to me I now consider loss for the sake of Christ. What is more, I consider everything a loss because of the surpassing worth of knowing Christ Jesus my Lord, for whose sake I have lost all things. I consider them garbage, that I may gain Christ and be found in him, not having a righteousness of my own that comes from the law, but that which is through faith in Christ—the righteousness that comes from God on the basis of faith.

—Philippians 3:7–9 NIV

---

[7] See also Matthew 1:21.
[8] John 8:34–36 NIV.

I particularly like how The Message translates verse 9: "I didn't want some petty, inferior brand of righteousness that comes from keeping a list of rules when I could get the robust kind that comes from trusting Christ—God's righteousness."

We are instructed here that there are two kinds of righteousness, the righteousness that comes from keeping the law and the righteousness that comes from personal reliance and trust in Jesus Christ. The first one depends on our own efforts and ability to do it right (self-righteousness); the second depends on Christ's ability to do it right (Christ righteousness). Self-righteousness is worked from the outside, while Christ righteousness is imputed to us as a free gift. The first fosters condemnation, pride, and insecurity; the second fosters righteousness, peace, and joy in the Holy Ghost.[9] Self-righteousness keeps us focused on ourselves and appeals to the human pride; Christ righteousness keeps us focused on Christ and leads to the death of self altogether.

We know from Scripture that no one except Jesus has ever been able to keep the law perfectly. "All have sinned and are falling short of the honor and glory which God bestows and receives."[10]

What solution did God come up with when He saw that we simply couldn't keep His commandments? Did He require that we try harder? Or did He say, "Away with you!"? How did God respond to our inability and failure to obey His righteous law? We can find the answer to this dilemma in Jeremiah 31:31–33.

---

[9] See Romans 14:17.
[10] Romans 3:23.

Behold, the days are coming, says the Lord, when I will make a new covenant with the house of Israel and with the house of Judah, Not according to the covenant which I made with their fathers in the day when I took them by the hand to bring them out of the land of Egypt, My covenant which they broke, although I was their Husband, says the Lord. But this is the covenant which I will make with the house of Israel: After those days, says the Lord, I will put My law within them, and on their hearts will I write it; and I will be their God, and they will be My people.[11]

The Lord simply annulled the first covenant as a means of righteousness[12] by fulfilling it Himself[13], then nailing it to the cross[14] and making a new covenant![15] One that would empower us to obey Him by writing His law within our hearts. He places His Holy Spirit within us. He gives us a new heart, a new nature, and a desire to do His will and to live righteously; and then He helps us do it.

In her book *In Pursuit of Peace,* Joyce Meyer describes a Christian as "someone who has had his heart changed by faith in Jesus Christ. He has had a change in his moral nature (See 2 Corinthians 5:17). He is not just someone who has agreed to follow certain rules and regulations and observe certain days as holy. Religion is filled with rules and regulations one must

---

[11] Jeremiah 31:31–33.
[12] See Romans 10:4 KJV.
[13] See Matthew 5:17.
[14] See Colossians 2:14.
[15] See 2 Corinthians 3:6.

follow to be part of a certain religious group. Christianity, however, is agreeing to follow the leadership of the Holy Spirit entirely."[16]

Those in Christ have chosen to submit to the leadership of the Holy Spirit completely and not to the demands of the law. Somewhere along the way, I realized that I had to take Him at His Word and that nothing other than entire reliance and dependence upon Him would ever work.

For years I wondered about Romans 8:1 KJV: "There is therefore now no condemnation to them which are in Christ Jesus, who walk not after the flesh, but after the Spirit." I just couldn't understand it. In the first part of the verse, God was telling me that there was no condemnation for me, but in the second part of the same verse He was telling me that if I walked in the flesh I was condemned. Well, I knew that I still sinned, not willingly, but I did sin; so didn't that mean that each time I sinned it was because I was in the flesh? Did it mean that I fell under condemnation each time I sinned? It seemed to suggest that I must be perfect all the time or I was in trouble. So much for trying to make me feel good with the first part of Romans 8:1, the second part canceled it all out!

One day I asked the Lord to explain to me what it meant, and He did. The revelation came while I was musing over Romans 8:1 KJV:

There is therefore now no condemnation to them which are in Christ Jesus, who walk not after the flesh, but after the Spirit.

---

[16] Joyce Meyer, *In Pursuit of Peace: 21 Ways to Conquer Anxiety, Fear, and Discontentment* (New York: Warner Faith, 2004), 31.

Then, my thoughts drifted to Galatians 3:3:

> Are you so foolish and so senseless and so silly?
> Having begun [your new life spiritually] with
> the [Holy] Spirit, are you now reaching perfec-
> tion [by dependence] on the flesh?

This is when the light went on. *Thank you, Lord! I get it!*
To walk in the Spirit means to live in dependence on the Spirit. And to walk in the flesh means to live in dependence on
the flesh. O what a revelation! This means that we are free to
depend on Him to perfect us, to make us what we ought to be,
to make us right! It means that we can now depend on Him to
mold us and to shape us into Christ's image. It means that we
can depend on Him to do the work in us that only He can do.
It means that we can depend on Him to complete that which
He started in us.[17] Condemnation pronounces us guilty and
brings a wedge between us and God. However, Christ is the
bridge to cross over to God. Accordingly, the Bible says that
we are to walk by faith and not by sight.[18] Therefore, receiving
the free gift of righteousness *is* walking in the Spirit. Trusting
Him to make us what we ought to be *is* walking in the Spirit.
Running to Christ for forgiveness when we sin *is* walking in
the Spirit. Trusting that we are saved by His grace alone
through faith and not relying on our human effort and ability
to make ourselves acceptable to Him *is* walking in the Spirit.

Consequently, anytime we submit ourselves to a law
and try in our own human effort not to sin is actually when
we walk in the flesh. It is so important for us to get this: as

---

[17] See Philippians 1:6.
[18] See 2 Corinthians 5:7.

born-again believers in Christ, when we allow ourselves to live under constant condemnation, we are living a flesh-led life, not a Spirit-led life. This is why it is crucial that we do not entertain condemnation, for the degree to which we surrender to condemnation is the degree to which we are walking in the flesh. Wow! When we are under condemnation, isn't it because we depend on our own strength to do it, but we fail? However, when we depend on God to do it, there is no room for condemnation, because we do not rely on ourselves but on Christ. Let us therefore make the distinction between a perfect heart and a perfect performance.[19]

We need to understand the difference between conviction and condemnation. You can know whether you are under condemnation or under conviction by the effect it has on you. Condemnation strengthens sin and keeps you in bondage to it so that you cannot get out. Condemnation keeps you in defeat. On the other hand, conviction brings with it the grace needed to overcome. You will never overcome sin by placing yourself under a load of condemnation; nor will you ever help anyone overcome sin by placing them under a load of condemnation. Doing so will only discourage them all the more and cause more damage. It is crucial that we understand it is the goodness of God that leads men to repentance, not His anger.[20]

Once I received the revelation on Romans 8:1, I went back and read Romans 8 again, but this time I read the whole chapter to also get the context. Look how the pieces of the puzzle come together now in light of what we just discussed. You can go ahead and read the whole chapter, but I want to

[19] See 2 Chronicles 16:7–9 KJV.
[20] See Romans 2:4 NKJV.

include here some of the key verses that are pertinent to what I am sharing with you.

> There is therefore now no condemnation to them which are in Christ Jesus, who walk not after the flesh, but after the Spirit. For the law of the Spirit of life in Christ Jesus hath made me free from the law of sin and death. For what the law could not do, in that it was weak through the flesh, God sending his own Son in the likeness of sinful flesh, and for sin, condemned sin in the flesh: That the righteousness of the law might be fulfilled in us, who walk not after the flesh, but after the Spirit. For they that are after the flesh do mind the things of the flesh; but they that are after the Spirit the things of the Spirit. . . . But ye are not in the flesh, but in the Spirit, if so be that the Spirit of God dwell in you. Now if any man have not the Spirit of Christ, he is none of his. . . . For whom he did foreknow, he also did predestinate to be conformed to the image of his Son, that he might be the firstborn among many brethren. Moreover whom he did predestinate, them he also called: and whom he called, them he also justified: and whom he justified, them he also glorified. What shall we then say to these things? If God be for us, who can be against us? He that spared not his own Son, but delivered him up for us all, how shall he not with him also freely give us all

things? Who shall lay anything to the charge of God's elect? It is God that justifieth.
—Romans 8:1–5, 9, 29–33 KJV

Alleluia! The fact that we have been freed from the law of sin and death frees us to walk in the Spirit. So really, walking in the flesh, as referenced in Romans 8:1, is walking under the law. But Christ came that we may be free from the law of sin and death so that we may be led by the Holy Spirit. Now that we have the Holy Spirit and we have been freed from the law, we are free to walk in dependence upon the Spirit of life where He works in us to mold us into the image of His Son. And because God is the one who justifies us, who is there that can bring a charge against us? It is God who justifies.

Let us therefore ask God to help us place no confidence in the flesh or in the law, and instead place all of our trust and confidence in Him.

[You] who are kept by the power of God through faith unto salvation ready to be revealed in the last time.
—1 Peter 1:5 KJV

Who Are You Anyway?

But when the time arrived that was set by God the Father, God sent his Son, born among us of a woman, born under the conditions of the law so that he might redeem those of us who have been kidnapped by the law. Thus we have been set free to experience our rightful heritage. You can

162

tell for sure that you are now fully adopted as his own children because God sent the Spirit of his Son into our lives crying out, "Papa! Father!" Doesn't that privilege of intimate conversation with God make it plain that you are not a slave, but a child? And if you are a child, you're also an heir, with complete access to the inheritance.

—Galatians 4:4–7 MSG

A few years after I was born again, God gave me a prophetic dream showing me the battle I would face with legalism. Please bear with me as I share this dream with you in detail and provide you with the interpretation as I have it today. Mind you, I did not understand most of the meaning of the dream until after He had already performed a great work of restoration from legalism within me.

In the dream, I was a high school student, and I was running late for my class. As I walked in the hallway of the school toward my classroom, an announcement was made through the school's speakerphones, and the lady said, "Kathleen Kaczmarek has been kidnapped!" I knew by the tone of her voice that the kidnapper was still roaming around and that he was a threat. But why had she said my name? I quickly became uneasy. Was it a prophecy of what would happen to me? Could there be someone else with the same first and last name? Hadn't it already happened? She said, "*Has been* kidnapped," but I was still there. When I reached the classroom, everyone was panicked. The teacher dismissed the class, and all the girls ran for refuge back home. The teacher left, everyone left, and I was left alone in the classroom. Suddenly I saw to my left maybe two or three strong men, muscle-bound men; and I started to look to them to protect me from the kidnapper. However, and to my surprise, even they ran for fear![21]

By now I was standing at the front of the classroom. On my right was a door that led to the hallway. At that moment, the kidnapper appeared in the doorway, laughed, and hid again. He wanted me to know that he wasn't far and that he knew where I was. I thought to myself "If even the muscular men can't save me, who can?" This is when the very voice of our heavenly Father spoke to me. I say our heavenly Father because when He spoke, His voice sounded like thunder. A fair description could also be like many waters. But I know it was powerful and loud and it resonated everywhere. I recognized it from the way it is described in John 12:29 where the Father speaks as a response to Jesus' cry to glorify the Father's name. The sound of His voice is likened to thunder. When the Father spoke to me, His voice seemed to be everywhere at the same time; it was outside of me, inside of me, went through me, and was everywhere! And this is what He said: "You are not alone, Jessica."

He didn't even know my name! But at the same time I knew that God obviously had to know my name. I didn't know what to make of it. I guess I had mixed feelings. Part of me was so blessed that God Himself would speak to me at this moment of great need in such a way, but at the same time I felt kind of offended that He didn't call me by my real name, Kathleen. That's the way the dream ended.

I had been spending some time searching the web for the meaning of the name Kathleen before I had the dream. I

[21] See Jeremiah 17:5 MSG.

also knew that my mom had debated between Kathleen and Jessica.

Most sites say that the meaning of Kathleen is "pure." Even a lady from church gave me a card with the name Kathleen on it and with a description of its meaning as "pure." Through my search on the internet, I also came across one site (and I cannot find the site anymore) where they insisted that even though most people say the meaning of Kathleen is "pure," it is a mistake. Instead it means some kind of dark sorcerer or something like that. I can't remember the exact words they used to describe it. Though I knew it was only a name and only one site, still it troubled me a little given my past and the way the Devil liked to play with my mind. Regardless, Kathleen represented who I was, in and of myself.

However, all of this didn't matter anymore after I had that dream because God had called me Jessica! So I hurried to the computer, eager to know the meaning of the name Jessica. I knew it had to describe how God saw me and that it represented who I was in Christ, for God had spoken it. When I found it, I was pleased to see that *Jessica* means "God beholds," "wealthy," and "foresighted."

Now, you may wonder where I am going with this. This part of this chapter is about our true identity, our new life, the one that is hidden with Christ in God.[22] The Bible says in 2 Corinthians 5:17 that if any person is ingrafted in Christ, he is a new creation (a new creature altogether); the old [previous moral and spiritual condition] has passed away and the fresh and new has come! This means that the past is gone. Who we were before is buried with Christ. We are a new crea-

---

[22] See Colossians 3:3.

tion. I believe that God is the ultimate visionary, and He has buried our past through the blood of Christ so that the new could come. Consider Abram, Sarai, Jacob, and Simon for example. Each of them were renamed by God Himself once they had an encounter with Him. Abram was renamed Abraham;[23] Sarai, Sarah;[24] Jacob, Israel;[25] and Simon, Peter.[26] In their days, names were very important because they represented who they were. See for instance the account where God changed Abram's name:

> When Abram was ninety-nine years old, the Lord appeared to him and said, I am the Almighty God; walk and live habitually before Me and be perfect (blameless, wholehearted, complete). And I will make My covenant (solemn pledge) between Me and you and will multiply you exceedingly. Then Abram fell on his face, and God said to him, As for Me, behold, My covenant (solemn pledge) is with you, and you shall be the father of many nations. Nor shall your name any longer be Abram [high, exalted father]; but your name shall be Abraham [father of a multitude], for I have made you the father of many nations.[27]

Just like God chose Abram, He also chose each and every one of us who are in Christ. God chose us and made us

---

[23] See Genesis 17:5.
[24] See Genesis 17:15.
[25] See Genesis 35:10.
[26] See Matthew 16:17–18.
[27] Genesis 17:1–5.

new creatures, children of God born of His will.[28] He gave us a new name representing our new identity in Christ Jesus.

I particularly like the account of Jacob in Genesis 32:26–28: "Then He said, Let Me go, for day is breaking. But [Jacob] said, I will not let You go unless You declare a blessing upon me. [The Man] asked him, What is your name? And [in shock of realization, whispering] he said, Jacob [supplanter, schemer, trickster, swindler]! And He said, Your name shall be called no more Jacob [supplanter], but Israel [contender with God]; for you have contended and have power with God and with men and have prevailed."

Notice what God gave Jacob as a response to Jacob's request to bless him. God didn't bless Jacob with more natural wealth or anything that this world could offer. How did God bless Jacob? He blessed him by making him a new man. How? He gave him a new name. He gave him a new identity. He gave him a new beginning. Isn't that glorious? Old things are passed away, behold all things are become new! We can be saved from our past! And our text in Galatians 4:4–7 is saying to us that we are the redeemed of the Lord, fully adopted as children of God, enjoying an intimate relationship with God by which we freely cry, "Papa, Father," and with complete access to our inheritance as rightful heirs. We are no longer under the law, but under grace, with free access to the Father and enjoying the peace of reconciliation with God through faith in Christ.[29]

Now, let me share something with you that I consider of utmost importance. What we believe about ourselves, how we see ourselves, and how we believe that God sees us is crit-

[28] See John 1:13.
[29] See Romans 5:1 AMPC.

ical. It will ultimately shape who we are and, really, the course of our lives. In Romans 6:11, the apostle Paul told us to consider ourselves dead to sin but alive to God. I heard Beth Moore say during an interview with Joyce Meyer what I consider to be one of the most powerful statements I have ever heard. It went something like this: "You will end up where you believe you belong. Always." The Bible says in Proverbs 23:7 that as a man thinks in his heart, so is he. We can put on a façade, but what we really are is what we think in our heart. This is why we need to renew our belief system with the truth of the Word of God. If we believe in our heart that we belong in the pit, no matter how hard we try, we will always ultimately end up in defeat. If we believe that we are a sinner, no matter how many good intentions we have, we will ultimately go back to the sin we are desperate to get free from. So it is important to believe with our heart that we belong to and with Jesus if we ever want to behave accordingly. It is important to believe what the Word says concerning us.

The Bible says about us that we are slaves of righteousness, not slaves of sin.[30] We are the righteousness of God through Christ.[31] We need to know this truth for ourselves: that we have been made righteous through Christ, that we are accepted in the beloved, and that we are forgiven.[32] Unless we see ourselves right with God through the blood of Christ, we will never be victorious and we will always end up in defeat in the end, always. Oh, there is such empowerment when we finally submit to the truth that we are new creatures in Christ, when we become single-minded regarding who we are in

---

[30] See Romans 6:18 NKJV.
[31] See 2 Corinthians 5:21.
[32] See 2 Corinthians 5:21; Ephesians 1:6 KJV; Matthew 26:28.

Christ and don't see ourselves as people who are bound and doomed to waver between two masters for the rest of their days in defeat. We need to see ourselves as people who love God and are devoted to Him, understanding that this was made possible through the finished work of the cross, having been given a new heart.

I am the handmaid of the Most High God, and He loves me passionately. I am His and He is mine.[33] I am His daughter, and I have received the spirit of adoption by which I cry "Abba! Father!"[34] I am dearly loved, the apple of His eye, a slave of righteousness, righteous to the core, a woman after God's own heart, someone whose heart hungers and thirsts after righteousness, concerned for other people.[35] And why can I say all of that? Because I stopped depending on my own strength to make it happen, and I now depend on Him to work it out in me according to His power at work within me.[36] I believe it was Billy Graham that said something that goes like this "I am not pretending, I am standing on God's promises."

We need to align our thoughts and our words with the Word of God if we ever want to see the manifestation of what is ours in Christ. We need to call those things that be not as though they were.[37] The Bible says that faith is in our mouth.[38] It is true that we need to believe now and let our feelings catch up later. It is true that we are more than our feelings

---

[33] See Song of Solomon 2:16.
[34] See Romans 8:15.
[35] See 1 John 4:16; Zechariah 2:8; Romans 6:18; 1 Samuel 13:14; Matthew 5:6; 2 Corinthians 5:14.
[36] See Ephesians 3:20.
[37] See Romans 4:17 KJV.
[38] See Romans 10:8–9 KJV.

and that we need to learn to live by what the Word of God says about us and not by how we feel about ourselves. If we won't do that, we will never rise above where we are currently. This is a choice that we must make: will I choose to believe what God says about me, or will I choose to believe what my feelings say about me? Will I live by faith (after all, aren't we *believers*?), or will I live by what I see? We are called to believe first, and then we will see the manifestation of what we believe later. I am not saying that we do not need to put any effort into it. No, for when we believe, we begin to walk accordingly. As you believe that you are righteous, you will begin to walk righteously. As you believe that the love of God governs your life and actions, you will begin to walk in love out of that belief. Depend on His Spirit to enable you and to lead you, and trust that He does.

As mentioned in chapter 1, in the summer that I turned eleven years old and ready for the sixth grade, we moved to Granby, Québec, and I had to go to another school. I was terrified because of the years of rejections I had already suffered through. The thought of moving from a small village to a town scared me even more. If I were rejected in a small village's school, it could only get worse in a "big" town's school. I still remember the first day. I had zero confidence in myself. I was sinking inside the closer I got to the school. I just didn't know how I would be able to face the students, but I also knew that someway, somehow I had to do it. This is when I decided to become someone else. As I walked toward the school, I decided I would live an act. I would be a character just like in a theatrical play. That way, someone else would face all the students and not me. The other me, the fearful me, I ignored. I acted daily, and this way of life became the norm.

Actually, it turned out that sixth grade was wonderful! I enjoyed it, I made friends, I loved the teacher, and I was even able to make people laugh during my oral presentations. I had a sense of humor. The other person, the one that was terrified, was buried and replaced with the new.

There came a time in high school when I didn't know who I was. It may be that the whole "becoming someone else" experience brought confusion surrounding my identity; I don't know for sure. It could very well be that the underlying unconscious questions were: Am I the old me or the new me? Who am I? Am I a mixture of the two? But one thing was for sure, I didn't know who I was. As discussed in chapter 1, knowing who I was, knowing my true identity, was like a black hole to me. A hole without a bottom. When I went to high school, the terrifying fear of being rejected popped its ugly head up and confronted me because, once again, I had to change schools. This is when I realized that my elementary school years had really played a major role in shaping me and they impacted me deeply. I was so nervous that, if I recall correctly, I even cried at school on the first day. I had such a horrible fear of man. Nevertheless, the new person was able to carry me through, and I ended up doing well in my relationships. Though the first day was rough, it wasn't a representation of how my high school years were going to be. They went well, I made friends, and I had fun. However, I was all too aware that my elementary school years impacted me significantly, and as a result I had developed a deep-seated insecurity.

Still, the decision I made that first day of sixth grade really served me well and spared me a world of misery. It enabled me to confront the world head-on for all of my remaining school years up to university. I don't know what I would have done without the new me, because the fearful me was shielded by her. The new person was the opposite of the old one. She was outspoken, she was social, and she didn't fear man. She had to be like that because that was her purpose.

Now, if an eleven-year-old girl can somehow get the revelation that one can simply choose in an instant to live as someone new, how much more are we, as children of God, enabled by the power of the Holy Ghost to live in the light of who the Word of God says that we are? As I mentioned already, there came a time when not knowing who I was caused great darkness in my life. However, we as children of God don't need to ever face such confusion, because God tells us who we are in His Word: a child of God, dearly beloved, the head and not the tail, above and not beneath, a chosen people, a royal priesthood, a holy nation, God's special possession.[39] All we need to do is believe it and begin to live as the new creation that we are in Him.

Your Breastplate of Righteousness

In teaching you about your new identity, I am also teaching you how to put on the breastplate of righteousness. Ephesians 6:14 KJV states: "Stand therefore, having your loins girt about with truth, and having on the breastplate of righteousness." There is no denying that we are in a war, a spiritual war. The Bible says that we wrestle not against flesh and blood but against principalities and powers in high places.[40]

---

[39] See John 1:12 KJV; Romans 12:19 KJV; Philippians 4:1 KJV; Deuteronomy 28:13 KJV; 1 Peter 2:9 KJV.
[40] See Ephesians 6:12 KJV.

The Bible teaches us that when thoughts, philosophies, and reasonings that are contrary to the Word of God begin to bombard our minds, we are to cast them down along with every imagination and every high thing that exalts itself against the true knowledge of Christ.[41] We need to reject every thought that does not agree with who the Bible says that we are, always and right away. We are taught not to allow even one such thought to remain. And we certainly can't entertain it, because we can't afford it.

We also read in 1 Thessalonians 5:8 that the breastplate of righteousness consists of two parts: "But we belong to the day; therefore, let us be sober and put on the breastplate (corslet) *of faith and love* and for a helmet the hope of salvation" (emphasis added). So we learn from 1 Thessalonians 5:8 that the breastplate of righteousness is twofold: faith and love.

It is of faith, because the righteousness that God prescribes is one that is of faith in Christ Jesus. We are made right with God freely through faith in the finished work of the cross.[42] We put on the breastplate of righteousness when we allow ourselves to believe this truth and when we live by this truth. It is the place where we have entered into the rest of God regarding our right standing with God, where we know that we are the righteousness of God through Christ, and where we know who we are in Christ. Not only do we need to know the truth about who we are in Christ, but we need to put on the truth; we need to live by it. If we truly believe we have been made righteous at the core and we are saints of God, we will begin to behave more and more righteously out of that belief. If we believe it, we will no longer live under the

---

[41] See 2 Corinthians 10:5.
[42] See Romans 5:16–17.

continual burden of condemnation. On the other hand, if we do not believe Christ set us free from sin, but rather believe that we are sinners, bound by sin, and bound to sin day in and day out, we will always end up sinning and opening the door to the Enemy through our lack of obedience to the law of faith.[43] As children of God, we need to choose which report we will believe. Remember that the law's job is to expose sin to us and to make us conscious of it.[44] So when we place ourselves under the control of the law, all it can do is condemn us. However, when the Spirit of God baptizes us (places us) into Christ[45] through our faith, the Holy Spirit Himself convicts us of sin in a way that leads to life, and He convinces us of righteousness.[46] Such work of the Holy Spirit in our lives is done without condemnation, and it empowers us to live righteous lives from glory to glory.

The second fold of the breastplate of righteousness is love. Love is a great spiritual protection from the Devil's schemes. Jesus said in John 13:34 NIV: "A new command I give you: Love one another. As I have loved you, so you must love one another." We are also instructed in Romans 12:21 AMP not to be overcome and conquered by evil, but to overcome evil with good. Love is a great defense. At its core, righteousness involves walking in obedience to God. Jesus said in John 14:23 that if we really love Him, we will obey Him. So when we love Him, we obey the voice of His Holy Spirit, and we wear the breastplate of righteousness. His

---

[43] See Galatians 3:1 KJV; Romans 3:27.
[44] See Galatians 3:19.
[45] See Galatians 3:27; 1 Corinthians 12:13.
[46] See John 16:8.

commandment is this: that we may love. Because He loved us first, it enables us to love.

A few years after I was born again, the Lord revealed to me that His body was handicapped. He showed me that His people's lack of obedience to the Spirit's promptings is a hindrance to Him; our lack of obedience to the Spirit disables Him. These are the words that the Lord spoke to me that night in a dream: "My people lose their authority because they do not obey the voice of the Holy Spirit." Please notice this suggests that the direct consequence of not obeying the voice of the Holy Spirit is not losing our salvation, but losing our authority. This has tremendous meaning. When we choose not to obey the leading of the Holy Spirit, we make ourselves vulnerable to the attacks of the Enemy through losing our authority. And as far as what we are talking about in this section, when we persist in walking in disobedience, we choose to put off the breastplate of righteousness which allow our most vital part, the heart, to become vulnerable to the Devil.[47] Again, out of our hearts flow the issues of life, thus the Bible tells us that above all else we are to guard our hearts with all diligence.[48]

You Are Not Alone

I want to elaborate on the kidnapping dream I had before I fell into legalism. If you remember, Kathleen Kaczmarek had been kidnapped. It was a few years after God had already performed a great work of restoration from legalism in my life that I heard Galatians 4:4–7 from The Message version of the

---

[47] See James 4:7; James 2:17; Ephesians 6:14 AMPC.
[48] See Proverbs 4:23.

Bible. Only then did I understand better the meaning of this dream. Please allow me to include it here again for your convenience:

> But when the time arrived that was set by God the Father, God sent his Son, born among us of a woman, born under the conditions of the law so that he might redeem those of us who have been kidnapped by the law. Thus we have been set free to experience our rightful heritage. You can tell for sure that you are now fully adopted as his own children because God sent the Spirit of his Son into our lives crying out, "Papa! Father!" Doesn't that privilege of intimate conversation with God make it plain that you are not a slave, but a child? And if you are a child, you're also an heir, with complete access to the inheritance.[49]

There we have it, plain and clear. The Lord was showing me that the law (legalism) would come and kidnap me, but that I could call to my heavenly Father and He would be strong enough to deliver and to protect me. The apostle Paul made it clear to us through Galatians 4:4–7 that we are not slaves, but children. Legalism reduces us to slavery through fear. However, God the Father has set us free from bondage to fear by adopting us as His own children through Christ.[50]

One particular night after God had delivered me from legalism, the Devil came to attack me. It really felt like a

---

[49] Galatians 4:4–7 MSG.
[50] See also Romans 8:15.

planned attack. This happened during the days where I grew stronger in my knowledge of who I am in Christ. It was very clear to me that the Devil was there and that he was running me through many of the lies, experiences, and places he had caused me to go through before—things which would have caused me to lose my confidence as to who I am in Christ. However, that night was different. I was confident within. I had no fear. It was as though Jesus and I were one. It was as though each time I rebuked the Devil, Jesus Himself were speaking through my lips. I resisted the Devil and never lost my peace that night. After the Devil ran me through all of his temptations and tests, it was as though I literally heard him say, "You are different." Alleluia! What victory! What a reason for shouting! Not that I haven't had times since where I have been shaken in my faith as to who I am in Christ, but that night was definitely a sign of growth and I praised God for it.

My brother, my sister in Christ, you are not alone! God the Father is more than willing and ready to help you come out of legalism completely, definitely, and permanently. Only cry out to Him, the God of your salvation, and see His mighty deliverance in your life!

Additionally, remember that in the dream He didn't address Kathleen, but Jessica. He addressed who I am in Christ; His very own daughter born of His Spirit, born of the will of God.[51] I do not claim to have a full grasp on this, but Kathleen, who I believe represents the old me, the natural me, the one governed by the flesh, was the one who was kidnapped by the law. Am I ever glad the Bible says it is no long-

---

[51] See John 1:13.

er I, but Christ that lives in me; and the life I now live, I live by faith in the Son of God who loved me and gave Himself for me![52] Jessica lives through our resurrected Lord. Kathleen, the old me, was crucified with Christ so that Jessica could be raised with Him unto newness of life.[53] And this truth goes for you too. The old you is gone; behold, the new you has come and lives in Christ our Messiah!

***

> For Zion's sake will I [Isaiah] not hold my peace, and for Jerusalem's sake I will not rest until her imputed righteousness and vindication go forth as brightness, and her salvation radiates as does a burning torch. And the nations shall see your righteousness and vindication [your rightness and justice—not your own, but His ascribed to you], and all kings shall behold your salvation and glory; and you shall be called by a new name which the mouth of the Lord shall name. You shall also be [so beautiful and prosperous as to be thought of as] a crown of glory and honor in the hand of the Lord, and a royal diadem [exceedingly beautiful] in the hand of your God. *You [Judah] shall no more be termed Forsaken, nor shall your land be called Desolate any more. But you shall be called Hephzibah [My delight is in her], and your land be called Beulah [married];* for the Lord delights in you, and your land shall be married [owned and protected by the Lord]. For as a young man marries a virgin [O Jerusalem],

---

[52] See Galatians 2:20.
[53] See Romans 6:4.

so shall your sons marry you; and as the bridegroom rejoices over the bride, so shall your God rejoice over you.

—Isaiah 62:1–5 (emphasis added)

CHAPTER 6
KNOWING GOD

O taste and see that the Lord [our God] is good!
Blessed (happy, fortunate, to be envied) is the
man who trusts and takes refuge in Him.

—Psalm 34:8

When I gave my life to God back in 2001, I was living in sin with Kurt. I wanted to move out of there as soon as possible, because I was now in love with Brian, plus I didn't want to live in sin. As a result, I broke up with Kurt and moved into the first bachelor apartment I could find. It was very expensive for a small bachelor apartment, but I really needed to move out as soon as I could, so I took it. Little did I know that one of the reasons why the apartment was so expensive was that a lady was employed to clean it once a week. I believe a few months went by and I had not given her any tips! I wasn't taught growing up the importance of giving tips so it didn't dawn on me that I should. But praise be to God our heavenly Father because He raises us up as His children indeed and teaches us in the way that we should go.

One morning as I was getting ready to go to work, minding my own business, God spoke to me. Of all my experiences with God, this one was probably the most amazing one to me. This experience was unique and probably the most beautiful one that I have experienced so far. That morning, I heard His voice as clearly as if He stood right in front of me. I heard the tone of His voice. It was in the spirit realm; I think that's why I could hear His real voice, His tone. I could hear *Him*. The very interesting thing is that His voice came from my own belly. This experience also reinforced the Word which says that He lives *in* us and that out of our belly shall flow rivers of living waters.[1]

These are the words He spoke to me: "Give her twenty dollars."

Now what happened next is somewhat comical, because I responded and said something like, "I don't want to give her twenty dollars. I don't even know if I have twenty dollars on me; and if I don't have it, I will have to go to the cash machine, withdraw money, come back, and it will slow me down for work!"

But that didn't keep Him from repeating the same words with the same tone of voice. "Give her twenty dollars."

To which I answered a similar song. "I don't even know if I have twenty dollars on me. And if I don't have it, I will have to go to the cash machine and come back. I don't want to be late for work."

To which He responded (you must have guessed it), "Give her twenty dollars," and with the same tone of voice. He didn't sound annoyed even the third time.

To which, praise be to God, I finally answered, "Okay, I tell you what, if I have twenty dollars in my wallet, nothing more, nothing less, I will know for sure that it is you and that you want me to give her twenty dollars, and I will give it to her." Of course, when I opened my wallet, there was one twenty-dollar bill, nothing more, nothing less. So I nicely put that twenty bucks on my living room table with a note stating that I was giving it to her. God knew her need, and God saw to it that He would meet it. But He also used this opportunity

---

[1] See John 7:38 KJV.

to bless me immensely by speaking to me the way that He did. Not only that, but God rewarded me financially only a few days later for being obedient to Him that day. Now I am sharing this story with you, because when He spoke to me, I clearly heard three specific aspects of His nature in His beautiful and winsome voice: I could hear His authority and majesty, I could hear His humility and meekness, and I could hear His love and compassion.

Knowing God's Nature

> In the year that King Uzziah died, [in a vision] I saw the Lord sitting upon a throne, high and lifted up, and the skirts of His train filled the [most holy part of the] temple. Above Him stood the seraphim; each had six wings: with two [each] covered his [own] face, and with two [each] covered his feet, and with two [each] flew. And one cried to another and said, Holy, holy, holy is the Lord of hosts; the whole earth is full of His glory! And the foundations of the thresholds shook at the voice of him who cried, and the house was filled with smoke.
>
> —Isaiah 6:1–4

How can I appropriately describe to you what I heard that day? The most majestic, most charming, most winsome voice of all. Song of Solomon 5:16 illustrates it so well: "His voice and speech are exceedingly sweet; yes, he is altogether lovely [the whole of him delights and is precious]. This is my beloved, and this is my friend, O daughters of Jerusalem."

The first characteristic of His nature that I heard that day was His authority, His majesty. His voice called for respect and awe, and His voice had all my admiration. His voice revealed His authority: an authority I desired in my own life. His voice was so majestic. I knew right away that a person of high rank was talking to me, and His voice perfectly suited who He is: the King of Kings and the Lord of Lords. He is our authority figure. As mentioned previously, the Bible says that the government will rest on His shoulder and to His kingdom there will be no end.[2] We are safe, as He has control over our lives.

We do deeply need and even desire someone to love us so much as to watch over us and put boundaries in our lives. You may have heard that children sometimes will test the boundaries because they want to feel secure. They want to know that their parents will always keep close watch over them and love them enough to never give up on them. The King of Kings and the Lord of Lords is our Redeemer, our Protector; and as our loving Father, He keeps a close watch over us and disciplines us for our certain good, that we may become sharers in His own holiness.[3] Praise God He loves us so and will not allow us to wander off where danger is without first warning us! He sets up boundaries for our best interest and for our protection.

---

[2] See Isaiah 9:6-7.
[3] See Hebrews 12:10 AMPC.

The Lord is humble and meek. God is the humblest being in the universe. The Bible refers to Him as the Lamb of God.[4]

> Come to Me, all you who labor and are heavy-laden and overburdened, and I will cause you to rest. [I will ease and relieve and refresh your souls.] Take My yoke upon you and learn of Me, for I am gentle (meek) and humble (lowly) in heart, and you will find rest (relief and ease and refreshment and recreation and blessed quiet) for your souls. For My yoke is wholesome (useful, good—not harsh, hard, sharp, or pressing, but comfortable, gracious, and pleasant), and My burden is light and easy to be borne.
> —Matthew 11:28–30

Our Lord's meekness and humility enable us to find rest in His presence even though we are far from being perfect. And it makes Him so worthy of all our praise! Unless He were humble, we would never be able to love Him with our whole heart because we would feel threatened and belittled by Him. And without humility there is no way He would have followed through at Calvary. We can feel safe in His presence just the way we are to the way where we are going, "for we do not have a High Priest Who is unable to understand and sympathize and have a shared feeling with our weaknesses and infirmities and liability to the assaults of

---

[4] See John 1:29.

temptation, but One Who has been tempted in every respect as we are, yet without sinning."[5]

My husband told me that one day the Lord spoke to him these very significant words: "I am the judge, but I am not judgmental." How powerful that is. I find this describes Him so well. Yes, He is the judge. But He is a merciful, understanding, and compassionate judge. He is a God of the heart; He knows our hearts, and we can find security in that when we find ourselves weak. He is meek and lowly in heart, and He seeks to give us rest as we surrender our lives to Him and find refuge in the safety of His embrace. Philippians 2:5–11 essentially tells us that although being one with God and equal with God in possessing the fullness of the attributes of God, He stripped Himself of all privileges and rightful dignity and assumed the guise of a servant (slave) and was born a human being. And even after He had appeared in human form, He humbled Himself even more and carried His obedience to the extreme of death, even the death of the cross. Because of that, God has highly exalted Him and has freely bestowed on Him the name that is above every name, that in the name of Jesus every knee must bow, in heaven and on earth and under the earth, and every tongue confess that Jesus Christ is Lord, to the glory of God the Father.

In my early years with the Lord, He allowed me to experience the manifest presence of His love. I was worshipping in my bachelor apartment (the same apartment I was living in when He spoke to me, "Give her twenty dollars") when suddenly His love manifested. When I experienced His love, the thought that came across my mind was this: *a man could go as*

---

[5] Hebrews 4:15.

far as to kill even three times and would never be able to come close to reaching the limit of God's love! And really, it doesn't matter how many times. The old song "The Blood Will Never Lose Its Power" best describes how I experienced His love. It was higher than the highest heights, lower than the lowest lows.

The Bible says that God is love and 1 Corinthians 13 describes what love is.[6] Reading 1 Corinthians 13:4–7 also helped me know Him and His nature. It helped me trust Him.

> Love endures long and is patient and kind; love never is envious nor boils over with jealousy, is not boastful or vainglorious, does not display itself haughtily. It is not conceited (arrogant and inflated with pride); it is not rude (unmannerly) and does not act unbecomingly. Love (God's love in us) does not insist on its own rights or its own way, for it is not self-seeking; it is not touchy or fretful or resentful; it takes no account of the evil done to it [it pays no attention to a suffered wrong]. It does not rejoice at injustice and unrighteousness, but rejoices when right and truth prevail. Love bears up under anything and everything that comes, is ever ready to believe the best of every person, its hopes are fadeless under all circumstances, and it endures everything [without weakening].[7]

This is who He is. This is how He is. This describes His nature perfectly. God is not self-seeking. God does not pay

---

[6] See also 1 John 4:8.
[7] 1 Corinthians 13:4–7.

attention to a suffered wrong. God endures long and is patient and kind. He is never rude. God is not touchy. Did you hear that? Read it again: God is not touchy. If you feel like God is displeased with the least little error or the slightest wrong thought, or because you gave in to a can of pop or a chocolate bar, then understand that this view of God is a distorted view. The Jesus you are fearing is in fact another Jesus, and the Devil has successfully painted in your mind the picture of a Jesus who is not the real one. Unfortunately, because you believed the lie, it has become your reality in the sense that you are now submitting yourself to this harsh, impatient, and hard-to-please god; and you are suffering the consequences of this wrong perception of the Lord.

Now, combine the three characteristics (authority, humility, and love) in one voice and tell me if you can resist such a voice. Wow, wow, wow! No, you can't and neither can I! I am speechless before such majesty, such beauty, such holiness, such meekness, such love. He is a treasure to be sought after indeed. He *is* heaven; He is what makes heaven heaven. In His presence there is fullness of joy; In His right hand there are pleasures forevermore.[8]

God practices what He preaches, and He leads by example. If He asks us to bear with the weak, it is because He bears with the weak.[9] If He tells us that love overlooks transgression, then He is more than ready to overlook ours.[10] If He wants us to forgive our enemies, then He is willing to do the same thing toward His enemies.[11] Mercy is undeserved, this is

---

[8] See Psalm 16:11.
[9] See Romans 15:1.
[10] See Proverbs 17:9.
[11] See Matthew 5:44.

why it is mercy. God loves mercy and He desires mercy over sacrifice.[12] The Bible says that while the blood of Abel cried out for vengeance, Christ's blood speaks of mercy, and that God didn't send Jesus to condemn the world, but that through Him the world may be saved.[13]

God is good. He cares about everything that concerns us. I'm reminded of this when I reflect on an experience I had while engaged to Paul. One afternoon he arrived at my house and I was struck by how awkwardly dressed he was. While I pondered about his ungainly appearance, he told me that he'd had his eyes tested. "I need glasses" he declared. All I could picture was Paul crowning his ensemble with a pair of big round glasses. That did it! I was boiling inside. *God! Why are you doing this to me? Why did you have to choose a man for me that I am not even attracted to? And now he needs glasses?* Today, I find Paul to be a fine looking man but somehow, before we were married, I wasn't especially fond of his appearance. Very soon after his declaration, I was riding on the subway still upset about the idea of Paul needing glasses. Suddenly, I had a vision; right in front of me was Paul. His head was sideways so that I could see his profile. He was wearing a pair of small, stylish rectangular-rimmed glasses. He looked good. Really good! The glasses Paul finally bought looked exactly as God had revealed to me. God cares about every detail of our lives. He is not just interested in the lofty spiritual matters, but even in the little things. God loves us and He cares about how we feel.

In his book, *Fiery Faith*, A.W. Tozer shares just how much he believes that our view of God's nature can significantly impact our soul. "Nothing twists and deforms the soul more than a low or unworthy conception of God." And "our notion of God must always determine the quality of our religion."[14]

There is one more trait of God's nature that I want to talk about—His holiness; God is a consuming fire. God loves us too much to leave us the way we are, to leave us unchanged. God cannot start the purifying work in us before He saves us. He saves us first and then He begins sanctifying us. One needs to catch the fish before he can clean it. It is important for us not to allow ourselves to feel condemned when the Lord shows us that something is wrong with us. How can we ever change and make progress unless the Lord first reveals to us that something needs to change? We need to be excited when the Lord shows up that way! Then like a child, His child, we do what He tells us to do, because we love Him and because He is God. We don't want to find ourselves outside of His will, because He is the God of the universe and being outside of His will would mean being outside of anything that makes sense and is worth living for. Apart from Him nothing makes sense.

The Bible talks about a baptism of fire.

> I baptize you with water for repentance. But after me comes one who is more powerful than I, whose sandals I am not worthy to carry. He will baptize you with the Holy Spirit and fire.
> —Matthew 3:11 NIV

---

[14] A.W. Tozer, *Fiery Faith: Ignite Your Passion for God* (Camp Hill, Penn.: WingSpread Publishers, 2012), 83, 84.

Not only are we baptized with the Holy Spirit, but we are also baptized with fire. As a consuming fire, in the times of chastening and because of His love for us, God will reveal to us our faults. [15] The Bible says that He will complete in us what He started and that He will perfect that which concerns us.[16] Another great promise is found in Jude 1:24, where it says that He is well able to present us blameless before the presence of His glory in triumphant joy. Therefore, we do not need to worry. If there is something that He wants to change in us, as the keeper of our souls, as our jealous God, and as the consuming fire of our lives, He will make it known.[17] Not only will God reveal to us when something is wrong, but He will empower us to make changes. For some sins, overcoming them is just a matter of realizing that we sinned and stopping them. Other sins may require some time, hard work through God, and patience if they have become strongholds in our lives.

God has always been very active in revealing to me when things are not right with me and in need of change. I know by experience and by the Word of God that He does not mince His words and He does not hesitate to let me know plainly when I am doing something that is displeasing to Him and in need of change. God shows me when I sin, and He persists until it is dealt with. Our earthly fathers disciplined us for only a short period of time and chastised us as seemed proper and good to them; but, as mentioned previously, God

---

[15] See Revelation 3:19.
[16] See Philippians 1:6; Psalm 138:8.
[17] See Psalm 121:5; Exodus 20:5.

disciplines us for our certain good, that we may become sharers in His own holiness.[18]

The good news is that when we become aware that we
sinned, we can receive immediate forgiveness and cleansing
through confessing our sin to God.[19] We also know from the
Word that those who belong to Christ have crucified their
flesh and its passion.[20] I love what Joyce Meyer says concerning this. She explains that the way to crucify the flesh is to
stop feeding it; anything that is starved ultimately dies. Isn't
that so true?

The Lord is a consuming fire. He can't help it; this is
who He is; this is His nature. The Lord is holy. The Word says
that the four living creatures never stop saying, "HOLY, HOLY,
HOLY [is the] LORD GOD, THE ALMIGHTY [the Omnipotent, the
Ruler of all], WHO WAS AND WHO IS AND WHO IS TO COME [the
unchanging, eternal God]."[21]

> His voice shook the earth [at Mount Sinai] then,
> but now He has given a promise, saying, "YET
> ONCE MORE I WILL SHAKE NOT ONLY THE EARTH,
> BUT ALSO THE [starry] HEAVEN." Now this [ex-
> pression], "Yet once more," indicates the re-
> moval and final transformation of all those
> things which can be shaken—that is, of that
> which has been created—so that those things
> which cannot be shaken may remain. Therefore,
> since we receive a kingdom which cannot be

---

[18] See Hebrews 12:10.
[19] See 1 John 1:9.
[20] See Galatians 5:24.
[21] Revelation 4:8 AMP.

shaken, let us show gratitude, and offer to God pleasing service and acceptable worship with reverence and awe; for our God is [indeed] a consuming fire.

—Hebrews 12:26–29 AMP

A few years after I was born again, the Lord gave me a dream which I believe will help us understand what this means to us, His children. In the dream, I was in a public building on what appeared to be the main floor. People were going about their own business when suddenly, a man standing on a platform started to spit out fire from his mouth. He had one purpose in mind, touch the people with the fire. Panicked, people began to run out of the building in all directions. However, somehow I knew this was a man of God and that whatever he was doing, it was from God. The fire represented God's judgment. I was also aware that no one wanted any part of it, thus they were running away as fast as their legs could take them. I thought, *If I run away too, this will mean that I literally choose to run from what God is doing. I don't want to run from what God is doing! So I guess if God is in it, then I want in no matter the cost.*

At that moment, I cried out to the man, "Hey, you! Here!" and pointed in my direction. Without *any* hesitation the man turned my way and started aiming the fire straight toward me. When the fire reached me, my body made a slight move toward the left in an attempt to escape. After all, can you imagine being burned alive? My spirit, however, determined to be in God's will, kept me there. I kept my body in that spot ready for whatever God had in store even if it meant judgment. To my surprise, the fire didn't feel too hot and it didn't hurt me. It was fairly comfortable actually. However, I began to notice the intensity of the fire slowly increasing as the flame kept touching me. When I felt the intensity reach a level where it was going to start to hurt, I stepped out of the fire. That was the dream.

Because the kingdom of God is in me, a kingdom which cannot be shaken, I was able to bear under the fire. We know that as children of God, the judgment of God concerning us is "righteous." We also know by the Word and through experience that sin can easily beset us. [22]

It is wise to face the truth about ourselves now instead of procrastinating. The Bible says in 1 John 3:2–3 AMP that the ones who hope to see Him, purify themselves:

> Beloved, we are [even here and] now children of God, and it is not yet made clear what we will be [after His coming]. We know that when He comes and is revealed, we will [as His children] be like Him, because we will see Him just as He is [in all His glory]. And everyone who has this hope [confidently placed] in Him purifies himself, just as He is pure (holy, undefiled, guiltless).

Notice that in this dream I had the free choice to come out of the fire anytime I wanted to. When it started to hurt, to my shame, I came out. During the time I had this dream, I was going through some pressure at work. Because of this pressure, I had begun to withdraw from what I believed to be

---

[22] See Hebrews 12:1 KJV.

God's will. God used this dream to reveal what was happening in my heart, and this caused me to ask Him to help me stay in the fire no matter how hot it became. Regardless of the situation, we can ask God to help us stick it out no matter how hard it gets, understanding that God will give us the grace to do His will if we trust Him.

Accordingly, 1 Peter 1:6–7 indicates that the genuineness of our faith will be tested and purified as by fire in order that it may redound to our praise:

> [You should] be exceedingly glad on this account, though now for a little while you may be distressed by trials and suffer temptations, So that [the genuineness] of your faith may be tested, [your faith] which is infinitely more precious than the perishable gold which is tested and purified by fire. [This proving of your faith is intended] to redound to [your] praise and glory and honor when Jesus Christ (the Messiah, the Anointed One) is revealed.

As followers of Christ, whether we know it or not, we are enrolled in the school of the Holy Ghost; and we know schooling always involves testing. There are seasons of testing; there are times when our faith is greatly tested through trials and through falling under divers temptations. One of the reasons why we are tested by God is to see if we understand what we have learned so far. If we pass the test, we are ready to move to the next level. However, if we fail, we need to take the test again. Testing does not seem joyous to us. Yet James said that we ought to rejoice when we find ourselves enveloped in all kinds of trials and fall into various temptations, because the trial of our faith works in us patient endurance which, when fully grown in our lives, makes us fully developed, lacking nothing.[23]

Joyce Meyer says something that goes like this "He burns everything that is not consistent with His nature and He sets on fire whatever happens to be left."

Knowing God as Father

Because you are his sons, God sent the Spirit of
his Son into our hearts, the Spirit who calls out,
"Abba, Father."

—Galatians 4:6 NIV

It may have been a year or two after I entered into my journey of recovery from legalism when I had the following dream. In the dream, I saw two amazingly beautiful houses. I am not sure if the man with me was a real estate agent, but he took me inside one of the houses to show it to me. When I got inside, I saw the owner of the house. Lo and behold, he was a well-known pastor who I also knew to be a strong advocate of the doctrine "once saved, always saved," a belief I do not share. The inside of the house was stunning. The details, the arts, it was something to behold! I also saw an open door, which was leading to the basement. I could see light coming from the basement, but we didn't go down the stairs to see it (though I really wanted to). Once the brief tour was over, we walked toward the front door to leave, when a woman

---

[23] See James 1:2–4.

showed up. It looked like she had been in the house all along, but we had not seen her somehow. I knew she was the daughter of the man who owned the house. I don't know if this man has a daughter in real life, but God wanted to teach me something that night. When I saw her, I thought, *She must be so secure knowing her father believes in the doctrine "once saved, always saved."* She looked so peaceful, serene, and secure, and I could really see it in her. I longed for such security and peace with God, a place where I didn't need to fear that I would be rejected based on my performance, on my failure, and on my shortcomings. I believe that through that dream, the Lord showed me that the way I could experience real peace and security without having to lean on the doctrine of "once saved, always saved" was by seeing God as my Father through my faith in Christ. The Bible says in Romans 8:15 NIV, "The Spirit you received does not make you slaves, so that you live in fear again; rather, the Spirit you received brought about your adoption to sonship. And by him we cry, '*Abba*, Father.'" Rightfully seeing Him as my Father was part of the solution.

Here is an illustration of how this revelation can help us on a practical level. One Monday at work, during a one-on-one meeting with my manager, I did what I considered afterwards to be an inconceivable thing. I deceived my manager into thinking that I had more work on my plate than I really had, all because I was trying to avoid having to help with one of our quarterly projects that I disliked. As a result, I became more and more uneasy as the day went by. Then bedtime came and I was really struggling. As I reflected on that meeting, it became obvious to me that I had indeed plainly deceived my manager. How could I have done such a thing? As I replayed the meeting in my mind, I could see that I had done it somewhat knowingly and deliberately too. I was dumbfounded. Oh, the distress that filled my soul! At that point, I believe it is safe to say that I had pretty much recovered from legalism, at least that's what I believed, and God had already given me all the revelations that I needed to keep me standing. I was doing well, and I had been experiencing freedom from legalistic inclinations. However, after that incident, even though I fought not to fall again, the fact I had done this thing somewhat deliberately got the better of me and made me lose my standing. I found myself struggling with legalism again. I was so troubled with this whole ordeal, and now I was down again. I really want to be loved unconditionally, but wasn't God "legally" obliged to reject me based on the fact that I had made such a gross, deliberate mistake? The more I thought about it, the more I lost my peace, and down I went.

The one thing that has echoed loud and clear in me throughout this whole journey has been the desperate desire to be loved unconditionally for who I am, just as I am. Nothing else has been able to fulfill me, not really. I so longed for unconditional love, and anything that threatened to steal it from me shook me to the core every time.

God, in His goodness, already had a plan of attack; and before I had even sinned against Him, He had already started to make provision. You see, the night before this incident, I was at church with the boys. Both of my sons treated me with such disrespect and were just not their usual self. Not that they are little angels, but I thought they had grown up enough to know better than that. Their behavior was so bad and so out of place. I scolded them sternly, and I was hurt by the disrespect coming from them. However, I never once thought,

Right now you have no part of me any longer until you repent and change your ways, and that better be fast! I never thought that. I never thought of abandoning them right there and then on the spot. What I did think, though, was that they were going to suffer the consequences of their actions and that they were going to be disciplined sternly. But never once did I contemplate renouncing them as a result of their extremely bad behavior.

First of all, I know that deep down they love me. Secondly, I knew that this was only a matter of needing to discipline them. This was not a case where they were making a statement through their actions that they were rejecting me as their mom and leaving me. This was just my children at their worst. Through this occurrence, God showed me ahead of time how He would respond to what I would do the very next day. Deceiving someone is not the kind of stuff that I wake up every day and plan to do. This was me at my worst.

Even though God had graciously provided a way out the night before, I was still shaken. So the next morning I turned on the TV to Joyce Meyer's program like I would normally do in the morning before I head for work. Joyce was referring to King David when he sinned against the Lord with Bathsheba, killed Uriah, Bathsheba's husband, and covered up his sin until God sent a prophet to his house to expose his evil deeds.[24] Joyce went on to say that even though God knew David was going to mess up the way he did, God still chose him because He knew David's heart; He knew that David had a heart after God; and He knew that He would be able to work His will through David. Joyce also added something

---

[24] See 2 Samuel 11 & 12.

like this: the one way to know how mature of a believer we are is to see how quickly we are able to get over our sin and to move on after we repent. I would like to tell you that I moved on quickly, but I think it probably took me a couple of months to get back on my feet again. I like how Derek Prince explains what I am talking about in his book, *By Grace Alone*.

> Here is a parable from contemporary culture that explains how this works. Today we use credit cards to make most of our purchases. We do not have the cash on hand, but we offer the credit card and it is accepted just as if it were cash. God has made His righteousness "credit card" available to us through our faith. Thus, when you fail in any situation, you have the privilege of just stretching out the Father's credit card and saying to the devil, "My faith is still credited to me as righteousness. God accepts responsibility for me even the way I am." When we do this we are relying continually on the grace of God.[25]

The following Scripture is such a blessing to me because it tells me how our heavenly Father deals with us concerning the sins that we commit. As our Father, does He reject us on the spot? Does He continue to love us, but not without a good spank? How does He handle us when we fail Him?

---

[25] Derek Prince, *By Grace Alone: Finding Freedom and Purging Legalism from Your Life* (Bloomington, Minn.: Chosen Books, 2013), 184.

I will be his Father, and he shall be My son.
When he commits iniquity, I will chasten him
with the rod of men and with the stripes of the
sons of men. But My mercy and loving-kindness
shall not depart from him, as I took [them] from
Saul, whom I took away from before you.[26]

So when we commit an iniquity, or in other words, when we
sin, God is saying that He will not reject us, but instead He
will chastise us just like any good father would. Notice too
that He didn't say about David's offspring "*if* he commits iniquity," but He said "*when* he commits iniquity." There is a
difference.

I remember an incident in my early years as a Christian. I was at work. A colleague and I were sending emails
back and forth calling each other names, just for fun. The third
or fourth name he sent me was "Fleur de Lys". My jaw
opened. *Fleur de Lys!* In shock, I went to his desk. "Fleur de
Lys! How did you come up with that name?" He responded
"It just dropped into my head so I wrote it and sent it to you".
Let's just say, Fleur de Lys was not at all like the other names
we had been exchanging. You see, God had called me Fleur
de Lys through tongues and interpretation of tongues that
weekend. Through that incident, I experienced the loving
chastening of our Heavenly Father. Being addressed as Fleur
de Lys was enough to get my attention and cause me to stop
all name-calling right away. But also in choosing the name
Fleur de Lys, God was adopting a loving tone. Daddy was

---

[26] 2 Samuel 7:14–15.

telling His beloved daughter to stop what she was doing and Fleur de Lys stopped right away.

God doesn't expect us to never sin. He knows better than that; He is not an unrealistic or unreasonable God. He knows our carnal nature, that's why He sent Jesus. Isn't that a freeing truth? Alleluia! No more do we need to be perfect! We can be comfortable to be just the way we are unto the way we are going because Daddy loves us; and if something displeases Him, He will chastise us, but He will certainly not remove His love from us. How glorious that is! The Bible says that He will preserve all those who love Him.[27]

> The sheep that are My own hear and are listening to My voice; and I know them, and they follow Me. And I give them eternal life, and they shall never lose it or perish throughout the ages. [To all eternity they shall never by any means be destroyed.] And no one is able to snatch them out of My hand. My Father, Who has given them to Me, is greater and mightier than all [else]; and no one is able to snatch [them] out of the Father's hand. I and the Father are One.
>
> —John 10:27–30

Knowing God as Lover

> For as a young man marries a virgin [O Jerusalem], so shall your sons marry you; and as the

---

[27] See Psalm 145:20.

bridegroom rejoices over the bride, so shall your
God rejoice over you.

—Isaiah 62:5

God is a jealous and impassioned God, the Bible says.[28]
And while some people may be unsure whether they like the
thought that God is Jealous, His jealous love is what really
began to convince me that He loved me with a personal and
passionate love—that He pursued me (even me!) and that my
distance from Him due to my submitting to another, the law,
made Him uneasy and caused Him to seek me (*me!*). I was
important enough to Him that He was disturbed when I was
far from Him. It's like He couldn't stand it! And what caused
Him to feel this way? His jealous love.[29]

God does want all of our hearts and not just a part.
When we begin to love other things more than Him, He becomes very perturbed; and it doesn't take long for Him to let
us know! If you are at all familiar with the Song of Solomon,
you will quickly notice that the Lord is a passionate lover.

Do you remember in chapter 2 where I shared that I
began to have recurring dreams in which I had sexual affairs
and was returning to my old lovers, even though married to
Paul in real life? Although I didn't like these dreams at all, I
was dreaming them once in a while. Then the frequency of
them increased until I was dreaming them almost every night.
Well, the nights I was able to sleep of course. Talk about being
pursued by God! He refused to just let me return to that old
lover, the law, without a fight. He didn't just say, "Bah, so
what? Too bad for you; you snooze, you lose! You are not

---

[28] See Exodus 34:14.
[29] See James 4:5.

worth pursuing, and I am not going to give you another thought. You are gone, stay gone. In fact, I hardly noticed. And I don't care, because you obviously didn't abide in my Word, and if you don't abide by the rules you are not worthy to be called my daughter anyway. Those I accept must be perfect in all their ways, and all I care about is whether you are performing perfectly. Apparently you are not, so goodbye. You were not good enough, wise enough, or discerning enough to avoid the snares of the Devil; so as far as I am concerned, you are not worth giving another thought."

I am so glad that this is not the attitude God has toward us. Quite the contrary. The Lord says in Jeremiah 3:14a KJV: "Turn, O backsliding children, saith the Lord; for I am married unto you." We see the analogy of a married couple and the exclusivity that is expected and due between the two. God is a jealous God and He wants our whole hearts. He will not allow anything else to have first place in our hearts, and He will not share our hearts with anything or anyone else. He desires us to love Him with everything that is in us and, in comparison, to hate everything else.[30] But He will work it in us as we trust Him to overthrow every idol in our lives. He is our heavenly lover, our heavenly husband, our heavenly bridegroom; and He desires faithfulness and loyalty from us and nothing less. He will not tolerate a rival. The fact that He pursued me even while deep in legalism and that once He found me, patiently worked with me toward complete freedom, really helped me trust in His faithfulness and His commitment to me. This is when I understood that He doesn't just go through the motions with us, and it helped me make Him

---

[30] See Luke 14:26.

my Rock and my Fortress. When no one else knew what to do with me, He stood by me. In my most sinful and pitiful place, there He was: Jesus, the Lover of my soul. Through the worst of all the storms of my life, as legalism got the better of me, Jesus loved me. Though I saddened Him, yet He remained a very present help in times of trouble.[31]

Not only is God our Father, our Lord, our Master, our Guide, our Friend, our Rock, and our Refuge, but He is also our Lover. Jesus as our bridegroom is the Lover of our souls and He longs for us with a holy desire. Song of Solomon 7:10 KJV says it perfectly: "I am my beloved's, and his desire is toward me." He seeks such that will worship Him in spirit and in truth.[32] We can experience a holy and sacred romance with Jesus!

I think I can safely say that God had already delivered me from legalism when the following happened. I was in the car, and I was once again being tempted with legalistic thoughts. I was also preparing to preach, and the message that was on my heart was essentially what I am sharing with you here, that is, portraying Jesus as the Lover of our souls. I had the Song of Solomon brewing within me at the same time; and I asked the Lord as I pondered on the passionate relationship between the bridegroom and the bride, "Isn't all that matters that we love you?" And just as I was asking Him that, I felt for a brief moment what I believed was the witness of the Holy Spirit in my spirit that went something like this: "What more could I really ask of you?"

It must have been either the first or the second year after I was born again, a friend of mine shared with me a dream

---

[31] See Psalm 46:1.
[32] See John 4:24.

that God gave her. There was a Christian friend of hers, kneeling down at the altar of a church, dressed in a white robe. Then a lady from that church approached my friend and told her, "Listen to her, she loves God." What qualified her friend for such a positive report from God? Her love for Him.

All that matters to Him is that we love Him. Everything else will naturally spring forth out of that love. I am not saying that everything we say will be accurate, but our hearts definitely will be. Didn't Jesus say in John 14:23 that if a person really loves Him, he will keep His Word and obey His teaching? So we see from this Scripture that all it takes is our love, because out of it will flow obedience. But if obedience is forced out of a sense of duty and obligation, then something is not right. I am not saying that we will never do something out of duty or obligation, there are times when we don't feel like doing something but we do it because it is right and it is our duty. But if that's all there is to our obedience, always a sense of duty and obligation, with no joy in our walk with God, then something is wrong.

The root of our obedience needs to be our faith in God and our love for Him.[33] I believe more and more that only my love for Him, rooted in His love for me, can be strong enough to keep me to the end and that only my love for Him will enable me to finish my course successfully. No amount of fear will equate or be as powerful and as effective in the keeping of my soul as a consistent love. When faced with the hardest choice—between God or our own life—I believe that not only the fear of the Lord but also our love for Him mingled with

---

[33] See James 2:17; James 2:26; John 14:23.

His grace and His love for us will empower us to follow through.

To think that He died for us! For you, for me! We have been set free to love Him. He wants to be on our mind. When I think now, I talk to Him instead. For example, if I feel hot, instead of thinking, *O it is so hot today!* I say, "O Lord, it is so hot today!" I got that from Joyce Meyer. That's the advice I heard her give one day. Jesus is not lukewarm about His relationship with us, considering He died for us. He is very passionate about us, and to think that He wants to spend eternity with us in close fellowship with us! Intimacy forever, always with us in constant communion. Shouldn't the only reasonable response be to love Him passionately in return? He wants us to hunger after Him just like He hungers after us.

I simply love the testimony a young lady shared with me a while ago at my church. She told me that one day she just started praying, and the Lord responded to her with these charming words: "It's a pleasure hearing from you." Can you imagine such a response from our Lord? Wow, wow, wow! What an intimacy, what a fellowship divine!

God wants us to enjoy Him and He wants us to enjoy the journey. The Lord spoke to me one night and showed me this truth. He didn't want me to be so caught up with all the duties of the work that I would miss the beautiful scenery on my way. I am privileged to be on this journey, and He wants me to enjoy traveling through this pilgrimage. However, it is hard to appreciate the journey when under the burden of legalism.

Knowing God as Father, knowing Him as Lover, and understanding His nature all are important revelations needed for victorious Christian living and to protect us from falling prey to the deception that legalism is.

***

I am my beloved's and my beloved is mine.

—Song of Solomon 6:3a KJV

CHAPTER 7
FREEDOM FROM FEAR AND ANXIETY

To be overcome with fear and anxiety is actually sin. This statement may shock you and perhaps even offend you. I know I was not impressed myself. After all, wasn't I the first one to want out? *I* was the victim here! I was filled with so much fear and anxiety while under the spell of legalism.

We may even feel like our fears are warranted, but God sees them much differently than we do. The Bible says that God's thoughts are higher than our thoughts and His ways higher than our ways. God is displeased when we shrink back in fear, because it exposes a lack of trust in Him.[1] You may say, well, how unfair that is! It's not my fault if I am afraid and anxious. I certainly do not want to be that way. It is so tormenting! I am the victim here, not the bad guy! Believe me, these thoughts crossed my mind too. However, fear shows a lack of faith in God, and only faith pleases God.[2]

The work that God has for us is that we believe in Him, a work that He also enables us to do.[3] I remember sitting in the doctor's office. I told her that I was suffering from anxiety. She asked "do you see yourself ever being free from it?" Everything in me wanted to shout a big "no!" However, purely on the basis of faith, I responded "yes." I understood that had I said no, it would have given strength to it and made victory over it that much harder to attain. Succumbing to fear is the opposite of exercising faith in God. In fact, when we entertain fear, we are exercising faith in the Devil's report. This is why we need to repent of our fears and anxieties and look to God

---

[1] See Hebrews 10:38.
[2] See Hebrews 11:6.
[3] See John 6:29.

to deliver us from them all as we cooperate with Him all the way. We believe first, the feelings catch up eventually. All the while we are right with God because we have repented.

To surrender to the wrong kind of fear is to bow down to another master, and it causes us to defile ourselves. We are called to bow only before Christ the Lord and to serve Him only, for like we have discussed already, He is a jealous God.[4]

The book *Freedom from Fear* says it accurately: "The fear of the Lord is the one fear that dispels all other fears."[5] One night, I was in church when suddenly tongues and interpretation of tongues were spoken. God spoke to me through the interpretation and essentially said "If you want to fear so bad, fear me!" The beauty of the reverential fear of the Lord is that when we have it, it causes great peace to invade our soul.[6] Cast, therefore, upon the Lord all fear, superstitions, and curses, and let Him deliver you from them all.

Fear of the Unpardonable Sin

Therefore I say to you, every sin and blasphemy [every evil, abusive, injurious speaking, or indignity against sacred things] will be forgiven people, but blasphemy against the [Holy] Spirit will not be forgiven.

—Matthew 12:31 AMP

---

[4] See Exodus 20:1–6.
[5] Neil T. Anderson and Rich Miller, *Freedom From Fear: Overcoming Worry & Anxiety* (Eugene, Ore.: Harvest House Publishers, 1999), 235.
[6] See Psalm 119:165.

I believe it was a year before the Lord showed me that legalism was a problem in my life, I was plagued with the fear of the unpardonable sin. I had so many blasphemous thoughts bombarding my mind. What made them so scary to me was that they were swear words against the Holy Spirit. I could see that fear had something to do in triggering them. Each thought would cause me to fear the unpardonable sin; after all, hadn't Jesus said that whoever blasphemes against the Holy Spirit will not be forgiven? It caused me much agony during that period. But it proved to be only the beginning of the misery I was about to enter into. This state I found myself in was a warning sign that something was wrong, because as children of God, we are not supposed to be in continual torment. As I look back, I know that the fear of the unpardonable sin was all part of the Devil's evil scheme. Legalism can even be an open door for such fear. Someone plagued with the fear of the unpardonable sin depends too much on what they do as opposed to what Jesus has done. Legalism opens the door to all kinds of fear, because in the flesh, what we want to do, we don't do, and what we don't want to do is what we end up doing.[7]

When I shared with my mom (she was a believer by this time) that these sorts of thoughts were coming into my mind and that I was very afraid because of them, she said, "Why do you even bother with them? You know that this is not your heart. I know that if I had such thoughts, I would just brush them off and move on!"

Loving Jesus with our hearts helps keep us from unwarranted and persisting fear. When we love Him deeply,

---

[7] See Romans 7:15–23.

and when *we know* that we love Him, thoughts like these won't bother us as much, because we know that they are not from our hearts. When everything we do is motivated by love for God and for others, condemnation will not easily have an entrance. Loving Jesus keeps us and protects us from many fears; you know it's not your heart; you know it's not you! Someone under legalism lives from the outside in. As such, they are so focused on the law they must obey that they struggle to serve Jesus in simplicity, from a heart of love. There must not be a blasphemous thought crossing their mind, regardless of their heart condition, or they are doomed. They do not know the heart of God, or at least, they no longer know Him the way they used to.

You also have to realize how powerful a tool this sort of fear is to the Devil in helping him defeat God's people. If you begin to believe you have committed the unpardonable sin, you will become hopeless and begin to give up, to return to your sins or, even worse, be utterly ruined. It will lead you down the path of destruction very fast. You have to be careful what you allow yourself to believe; consider the end of result of what you choose to believe. The Devil wants you to be hopeless. However, the Bible shows that God is the hope to the hopeless.[8]

It is important for us to understand the whole counsel of the Word of God; yes, it is possible for someone to commit the unpardonable sin, but this truth need not contradict the other truths of the Word. For instance, Jesus said that He will in no wise reject those who come to Him.[9] This means that if you still want Jesus, if you still want to have a relationship

---

[8] See Isaiah 61:3.
[9] See John 6:37.

with Him, if you want to serve Him and to live for Him, then you have not committed the unpardonable sin or you would not have such desires.

There were times when everything in me would cry out: God has condemned you! He has rejected you! He has spoken woe on your life! During those times, I would take this Scripture: "Against hope believed in hope."[10] God being against me for sure met the requirement of *"against hope* believed in hope." I would also remind myself that He is the hope to the hopeless, which meant that He would be the solution to rid me of all of my fears even if those fears concerned Him. In fact, the Bible says that God is able to deliver us from *all* of our fears, not just a few but *all*.[11] The thought of His nature, His great love for us, and that He is a savior at heart also helped disarm such fearful thoughts. Because God was to be my helper, I began seeking Him. I was in so much inner turmoil that I asked Him to deliver me from those thoughts and from my fears.

As a result, He gave me a dream one night. In the dream, the evangelist Jesse Duplantis was a pastor of a church. There was this lady who kept judging and criticizing him. I was aware that this lasted for a long time, maybe many months or more. She constantly found something to say against him and didn't hesitate to openly share what she thought of him. Then she would come back the next week and the next week and the next week and do the same thing: condemn the man. However, one day, she came, as was her custom, but instead of saying something against "Jesse," she said something against *"Pastor* Jesse." The moment she spoke

[10] Romans 4:18 KJV.
[11] See Psalm 34:4.

against *Pastor* Jesse, she was gone. There was no more sign of her. And that was the dream.

God was showing me how someone can commit the unpardonable sin. As long as she criticized and spoke against the man himself, she was fine, but the moment she spoke against the office, the mantle, in other words, the moment she spoke against the anointing, she was no more. This dream set me free from that irrational fear. I realized that involuntary blasphemous thoughts against the Holy Spirit crossing my mind (though they certainly felt voluntary at times as fear tricked me and got the better of me) didn't really fit the description provided to me by God in the dream. God had showed me that the way one can commit the unpardonable sin is when they speak against the anointing resting upon a minister of God. Not only that, God showed me that committing the unpardonable sin doesn't happen overnight. But if one will keep playing with fire, keep disobeying God by devouring others and by slandering the ones God has placed in authority over them, then one has to be careful that he does not touch the anointing. It is preferable to leave all men and women alone, to leave them with God, and to pray for them with a sincere heart and a humble mind. The apostle Paul said in Romans 14:4 that to his own master a servant will stand or fall. And he added that indeed, he will be made to stand, for God is able to make him stand. Therefore, let's be imitators of King David who had King Saul at his mercy and chose not to kill him, saying to himself, "Do not touch God's anointed and do His prophets no harm."[12]

---

[12] See Psalm 105:15.

Fear of Failure and of Being Imperfect

The Lord will perfect that which concerns me; Your mercy and loving-kindness, O Lord, endure forever—forsake not the works of Your own hands.

—Psalm 138:8

I trust that what you have read so far already helped you with this kind of fear. I do want, however, to add one more thing that I believe will also help you rid yourself once and for all of such fear. One of the greatest benefits of being children of God is that we have been freed from having to be perfect in our performance. Perfectionism is a major hindrance to progress. The fear of failure and of being imperfect is a true sign that there is something we do not understand in the sound doctrine of the gospel. The Bible says that we enter into the rest of God once we place our faith in God.[13] It is important to be honest with ourselves and with God and to not hide in fear. If you struggle with such fear, remember you can ask God to reveal to you the root cause of your problem. Then, with God's help, you are enabled to deal with it. It is likely that you haven't understood fully the finished work of the cross.

Legalism always demands you to be at a higher level of holiness than where you are now. You may be at level three in love and level one in faith, but legalism is not satisfied, because you should be operating at level seven and eight, or actually you should be operating at level ten! It always brings

---

[13] See Hebrews 4:3.

the sense that you are not enough. It is a merciless place, a place where there is no life, no color, and no joy.

Jesus did not waste any words when He addressed the perfectionists of His day. Here is an excerpt of Jesus' blunt words in Luke 11:46: "But He said, Woe to you, the lawyers, also! For you load men with oppressive burdens hard to bear, and you do not personally [even gently] touch the burdens with one of your fingers." In contrast, grace will take us as we are and will help us make progress. Under grace, it is understood that the change will happen over a period of time and not all at once. If it were not so, a genuine work of the heart wouldn't be possible.

Consider again what James said in James 3:1–2: "Not many [of you] should become teachers (self-constituted censors and reprovers of others), my brethren, for you know that we [teachers] will be judged by a higher standard and with greater severity [than other people; thus we assume the greater accountability and the more condemnation]. *For we all often stumble and fall and offend in many things. And if anyone does not offend in speech [never says the wrong things], he is a fully developed character and a perfect man, able to control his whole body and to curb his entire nature*" (emphasis added). Obviously it looks like we are not perfect or James would not have written verse two!

During my recovery from legalism, when I was in prayer, I asked the Lord, "How can you love us so much when we are so messed up?" Immediately the Lord spoke to me as a word came to me from my spirit. The word was *hunger*. God is not looking for perfection. What God is looking for is hunger—hunger for Him, hunger for righteousness. Jesus said in Matthew 5:6 KJV, "Blessed are they which do hunger and thirst after righteousness: for they shall be filled." Therefore, let us pursue holiness with our whole heart and let us hunger for righteousness, but let us not forget that what God is looking for first and foremost is hunger, not perfect performance.

The Bible clearly shows that the merciful will receive mercy.[14] Like we already discussed, if there is room for us to receive mercy, it is because we are not perfect, or else mercy wouldn't be needed. I have heard it said, and I would have to consent, that if God were to show us everything that is wrong with us now, we probably would fall dead. We wouldn't be able to bear it. Again, let us make the difference between a perfect heart and a perfect performance. God has called us to enjoy the journey while we are on it. Philippians 4:4 tells us to rejoice in the Lord always (delight, gladden yourselves in Him), for He promised to perfect that which concerns us. He who has called us unto Himself is faithful; He will hallow us and keep us.[15]

The Selfishness of a Performance-Based Mentality

For the love of Christ controls and compels us, because we have concluded this, that One died for all, therefore all died; and He died for all, so that all those who live would no longer live for themselves, but for Him who died and was raised for their sake.

—2 Corinthians 5:14–15 AMP

[14] See Matthew 5:7.
[15] See 1 Thessalonians 5:24.

A year or two before the Lord showed me that legalism was my problem, I sought the Lord because I was really not well; I was very anxious, but I did not know what the cause was. My husband prayed and fasted for me. This is when the Lord spoke to him the word *epiphany*, revealing to us that God would come through for me through an epiphany, through a revelation. That very night the Lord gave me a dream. In the dream I saw a young nurse dressed in her typical white attire in what seemed to be a little kitchenette reserved for the employees who worked in that hospital. The nurse was fairly new in the hospital and was learning. An older woman was there with the young nurse, and she seemed to be either her supervisor or at least an experienced nurse or manager who was there to guide the young nurse and teach her what to do. The older woman asked the young nurse to pour some water in a glass for one of the patients, a man. The young nurse proceeded with the request and began pouring the water in the glass, but she was trembling so much that I was concerned the water would be spilled in the process. I felt sorry for her. I couldn't wait, for her sake, for her to have settled down in her new job so she wouldn't be so nervous. The dream ended like that.

I pondered the dream the next day. Surely it was from God and He was trying to show me something. However, I could not make much of it at first and was tempted to just give it up. But no! This dream was from God and I needed to find out what it meant. As I prayerfully went over the dream again, this is what I saw. The young nurse who was called to care for the patients was more concerned about her own performance than for the well-being of her patients. Because of that, she was self-conscious, and it made her shake even in doing a very simple task that was well suited to her level (beginner) and definitely not too hard for her to do. It was her self-consciousness and self-centeredness that made her nervous and anxious on the job. Instead of being filled with love and care for the suffering man who needed water, she was filled with selfish, self-centered thoughts of how important it was for her to perform well in others' eyes. She should have been doing what she really was called to do, which was to care for the ones who were in bad shape. What that patient needed at that time was not someone busy making sure she looked good and performed beautifully in front of others, but someone who cared for him during this very difficult and vulnerable time of his life. Had her focus been in the right place, her eyes on the patient instead of on herself, it would have protected her from anxiety and fear all together. Unfortunately the nurse, who represented me, was so caught up with a performance-based mentality that her heart of love for the wounded had been replaced with self-centered love for herself.

One of the churches my mother attended organized one-on-one teaching sessions, and she started participating. This took place maybe halfway through my recovery process from legalism. The lady my mom was teamed up with was going to be a mentor to my mom. Somehow, the teaching never really started, but the lady did manage to go out of her way a few times to help my mother out because my mom did not have a car back then. So the woman would help my mother go around and do errands and things like that. At some point she said to my mom something like, "I feel you have to teach me and not the other way around." She went on to explain to my mom that she felt that the one on ones were too

hard for her and she wasn't measuring up. She then an-
nounced she wouldn't do them anymore, to which my mom
agreed. But the weird thing, according to my mom, was that
after this conversation took place, the help stopped. My mom
thought it was strange until she realized that the lady had
been helping her because she was doing her good works. She
had good intentions, but she was doing good works in order
to conform to what she felt was expected of her, in order to
meet what she thought were God's expectations as well as the
church's. All the while, my mom thought they were develop-
ing a real friendship, when in fact the lady was doing her religious duties in order to measure up. She didn't help with a
sincere heart toward my mother, but instead she sought to
meet religious standards and expectations, some sort of a religious system. My mother concluded, "It was not really friendship, and it was not real."

The day came when my mom felt led to leave that
church. She said that after she left, she did miss one man. She
knew he was sincere. They would fellowship outside the
church heart to heart about the Lord and about their experiences with Him. She knew he didn't talk with her because he
was under a duty to love her. No, he wanted to talk with her,
and he enjoyed the conversation. The result was she missed
him.

A word to spiritual leaders, let us be careful when we
create programs that we do not fall into the trap of going
through the motions. We feel it when someone is sincere,
don't we? Authenticity is what we are looking for as human
beings, but most of all, authenticity is what Jesus is looking
for. We have to remember that we are dealing with people
with hearts and feelings. God saved us and poured His unde-

served favor upon us to set us free from religion and from the "must do this and must do that." He has set us free from dead works so that we can serve Him in sincerity of heart.[16]

> Many false prophets will appear and mislead many. Because lawlessness is increased, the love of most people will grow cold.
>
> —Matthew 24:11–12 AMP

About two or three years into my recovery from legalism, the Lord gave me a dream. A minister's conference was going on. The room was circular so that the pulpit and the altar were situated at the center of the room. As I looked around, the ministers were all dressed in their best outfits—suits, ties. The service had just ended and an altar call was given. One woman came to the altar because she needed help and needed someone to minister to her and to pray for her. Though the entire room was filled with ministers, only one person went to minister to the woman. This is when my older son, Aaron, appeared and said, "The kingdom is finished." That was the essence of the dream.

What made Aaron's statement so shocking is that Aaron has had a speech impairment since he was really young, which has made it hard for him to speak smoothly and with ease over the years. However, in the dream, Aaron spoke without any struggle; he spoke perfectly, freely, and soberly. This reinforced to me that God's anointing was upon Aaron when he spoke these words. At the time I had the dream, Aaron was probably about nine years old.

---

[16] See Hebrews 9:14.

Now, I cannot tell you that I have the full understanding of what this dream means. However, I know the context in which these words were spoken. Whether God is saying that the selfish, self-centered kingdom of man is done away with or that the kingdom of God is finished, that is, it has stopped bearing the fruit that it was intended to bear on the earth due to our self-seeking ambition in ministry, I do not know. However, I do know that it is important for us to remember our original call from Jesus, which is found in John 15:12: "This is My commandment: that you love one another [just] as I have loved you." Let us therefore earnestly pray to God that we may genuinely grow in the love of Christ by God's grace and mercy.

I believe it was not long after the Lord had showed me that legalism was my problem, I was lying on my bed. I was in such a terrible state. I had come to the place where I even feared fear. So fear kept creeping up on me because I feared it. Panic attacks were always at arm's length. I really reached a place of hopelessness there, because I felt that if I feared fear, how was I ever going to be free from it? I was helpless. Fear had won over me. I didn't know how one could ever be rescued from such darkness. This is when it dawned on me how selfish this place was. If I were going to allow myself to stay there, I would always be in a surviving mode, a self-protecting mode. I would always be self-centered. My whole world would revolve around me, because I would be in constant need of help, feeling constantly threatened. This is when I realized that the way out was wrapped up in the decision to get out. I decided that for the sake of others and for the sake of not living a selfish life, I was no longer going to fear fear.

As we begin to die to self, these kinds of fears will lose their hold over us. Not only that, but dying to self will prevent them easy access in our lives, because they will have no appeal to us anymore. There will be no more "self" to protect, because "self" will be dead, crucified with Christ.

> Since by your obedience to the Truth through the [Holy] Spirit you have purified your hearts for the sincere affection of the brethren, [see that you] love one another fervently from a pure heart.
>
> —1 Peter 1:22

Freedom in Loving Others

> For God has not given us a spirit of fear, but of power and of love and of a sound mind.
>
> —2 Timothy 1:7 NKJV

It had only been a few days since God had spoken to me these words as a response to my cry for deliverance and for guidance: "What must one do to go to heaven?" Though God had informed me of the way out of legalism, becoming like a little child again, I was far from having arrived by the moment He asked this question. So maybe a couple of nights after that, a feeling of terror woke me up; and a weird, robotic, female voice spoke. It said, "I am afraid."

That next morning, I pondered what had happened that night. Standing in the washroom, I exclaimed, "What was that?"

No sooner had I asked the question I heard the Lord say: "Go love on someone else and it will leave you."

Surprised, I repeated the words. "Go love on someone else and it will leave you? I don't understand, Lord. I don't understand the connection." I knew I would find the answer in Scripture, so I tried to recall Bible verses that would shine some light on the Lord's statement. I quickly remembered these two Scriptures: "For God has not given us a spirit of fear, but of power and of love and of a sound mind"[17] as well as "perfect love casts out fear."[18] This was it! Oh my! Wow, Lord!

The Lord's powerful statement revealed to me a couple things. First, there is indeed such a thing as a spirit of fear. When the Lord spoke, He said, "And *it* will leave you." Second, I didn't have feelings of love flooding my soul for anyone when God spoke to me; I was full of fear! This suggests that we do not need to wait for feelings to show up before we start loving others. Instead, loving others consists of actions born out of a decision that we make in obedience to the Lord.

That day, by faith, I called someone in need and ministered to her. I loved her in action as I ministered to her the best that could with a sincere heart. By the end of the day, the spirit of fear was gone. I would love to tell you that it never came back, but I have had to fight against that spirit numerous times. However, the Lord taught me that day a way of living, a new lifestyle whereby as we abide in it more and more, the spirit of fear will have less and less entrance into our life. That way of life is love. He also taught me that love is one of our greatest spiritual protections in this spiritual warfare.

---

[17] See 2 Timothy 1:7 KJV.
[18] See 1 John 4:18 NKJV.

It is wise to love, and without love, we will be miserable. But love will cost us something. It usually involves some sort of sacrifice, but from experience I know that not walking in love will cost us more. It will cost us our joy, our peace, and ultimately our victory. Have you lost your joy? It could be that you need a deeper love walk. One of the best ways in the kingdom of God to invest in ourselves wisely is to lose sight of ourselves and to take care of the needs (spiritual, emotional, physical, financial, etc.) of others. This way, we build treasures in heaven that no moth can destroy.[19] If you really want to take care of yourself, take care of others also. As we take care of others' needs, God will take care of ours.

Love is a mighty spiritual weapon and is a powerful spiritual force. Consider the apostle Paul. He was filled with so much love for his own kinsmen that he wished he was cursed himself instead of them![20] Let us take ourselves off our minds by casting our cares on God, and let us go and love on someone else.

Jesus described a practical way to overcome anxiety in Matthew 6:31 KJV, where He says, "Therefore take no thought. . . ." Once we confess our sin to God, it is cleansed by the blood of Christ; and we can stop thinking about it from that moment on because it has been dealt with. The same is true about all of the cares we carry; once we give them to God, we then take no thought about them anymore because they are taken care of by our Father in heaven. When we get ourselves off of our own deficiencies, we get happy because we don't have so many cares and anxieties to deal with anymore. Anxieties and fears are there when we have ourselves and our

---

[19] See Matthew 6:19–21 KJV.
[20] See Romans 9:3.

own well-being on our minds all the time. A triumphant life cannot really be ours unless we learn to love one another. And we find freedom when we begin to operate in the new life-style Jesus offers us: love.

God Will Use It for Good

And we know [with great confidence] that God [who is deeply concerned about us] causes all things to work together [as a plan] for good for those who love God, to those who are called according to His plan and purpose.

—Romans 8:28 AMP

The Lord in His mercy and in His foreknowledge gave me a dream a few years before I plunged deep into legalism. In the dream, I was in a resort of some sort. It was made known to us (the people staying at the resort) that a man had just fallen. Then a woman whom I didn't see but heard said to me, "This will happen to you too." After she spoke these words, I began falling from where I was standing. I didn't really see where I was standing; but I knew it was at a higher level, because I felt myself falling for a good distance before landing on the ground. After the fall, the perspective of the dream changed so that I now could see myself just as if I were watching a movie. The scene was a little disturbing because I saw myself with only one eye. The other eye was gone! What was left was just the empty eye socket. People began to express a great sigh of pity for me, to which I responded, "No, don't feel sorry for me. This was the best thing that has ever happened to me." By then I was wearing a white robe. There

226

was such serenity about me, oh, a serenity and a peace that I had longed to experience for so long. Now keep in mind that I was watching as a spectator. It is then that I arrived at the edge of a pool of water. I was at a higher altitude from where the pool of water was. It was made known to me that the water was sick. Without hesitation I jumped in the water to save the water because the water was sick. That is the way the dream ended.

I debated whether I should include this dream in this book for difference reasons, but I believe it carries tremendous meaning; so by faith, I have included it here.

Having a single eye speaks of being single-minded. Jesus said that if our eye causes us to sin, to pluck it out. Sometimes, it takes something as drastic as a fall to cause us to make up our mind as to what we will believe and whom we will serve. I know from my own experience and from the Word of God that we cannot stand for very long if we are double-minded; we need to set our mind and keep it set.[21]

I believe that the pool of water represented a pool of people, a part of the body of Christ which is sick due to legalism and in need of healing.

God was not surprised by my struggle with legalism and He sought to use what I had gone through for good. He desired to set me free from its spell and purposed to make me able to help others who are suffering from the same thing I suffered from. One of the reasons God allows His people to go through hardship is to enable us to, in turn, help others who are suffering in the same way. Second Corinthians 1:3–4 AMP illustrates this thought very well: "Blessed [gratefully

---

[21] See Colossians 3:2.

praised and adored] be the God and Father of our Lord Jesus Christ, the Father of mercies and the God of all comfort, who comforts and encourages us in every trouble so that we will be able to comfort and encourage those who are in any kind of trouble, with the comfort with which we ourselves are comforted by God." Throughout my battle with legalism, I had an intense desire to one day help other people who suffer from the bondage of legalism. I also had a strong desire to help people who have serious problems with their mind in general. I had a fixed vision that the Lord would one day use me in this way. Simply put, I had you in mind during my whole journey to complete recovery. God will move heaven and earth for someone who wants to be free, not only for themselves but also for the sake of others.

One night, a few years before I completely fell into legalism, the Lord woke me up at three o'clock in the morning with an audible voice. This was my first time hearing God speak to me with an audible voice. But the thing too is, it was three o'clock in the morning! Woke me up! I mean this had to be important. *Serious* business. And these are the words that the Lord spoke to me that morning: "You have to be willing to be bleeding for the sake of others."

The next day I had the television on with a Christian program airing. I was in the kitchen doing I don't remember what, when I heard the preacher say, "You have to be willing to be bleeding for the sake of others." Oh my goodness! To this day I wish I had been sitting right in front of the TV screen to be double sure that I heard correctly. I have thought more than once that maybe I should have called the program to ask them to send me the tape just to confirm.

God allowed me to bleed as I suffered exceedingly at the hand of legalism and was greatly wounded as a result so that He could in turn rescue me, heal me, and ultimately use it for the greater good. By the same token, God will use what you are going through for good, and nothing will be wasted. He has a purpose and His will is always good, we need only to trust Him all the way, knowing that what the Devil means for evil, God means for good.[22]

---

[22] See Genesis 50:20.

CHAPTER 8
SERVING GOD

The Law of Faith

To declare, I say, at this time his righteousness:
that he might be just, and the justifier of him
which believeth in Jesus. Where is boasting
then? It is excluded. By what law? Of works?
Nay: but by the law of faith. Therefore we con-
clude that a man is justified by faith without the
deeds of the law.

—Romans 3:26–28 KJV

This is it. The law of redemption is the law of faith. It is
faith in the finished work of the cross; it is believing in Jesus
as our Lord and our Savior. Everything else (longing of the
heart, works, deeds) will naturally flow from that faith and
will be acceptable to God, having been purified by the grace
of God through faith. How did the apostle Paul respond to the
jailer when he asked him the most important question that
can be asked on this planet?

But Paul shouted, do not harm yourself, for we
are all here! Then [the jailer] called for lights and
rushed in, and trembling and terrified he fell
down before Paul and Silas. And he brought
them out [of the dungeon] and said, men, what
is it necessary for me to do that I may be saved?
And they answered, believe in the Lord Jesus
Christ [give yourself up to Him, take yourself
out of your own keeping and entrust yourself

231

into His keeping] and you will be saved, [and this applies both to] you and your household as well.[1]

"Believe in the Lord Jesus Christ and you will be saved." Please note that the apostle Paul wasn't apologetic in his response. He did not hesitate to give the *one* criterion: believe. To which you may say, You mean, that's it? There is nothing else required to save my soul? Nothing else is needed to make me acceptable to God? I don't have to do anything? I don't have to earn my salvation in any way shape or form? Are you telling me that I can just receive it as a free gift where it does not depend on me? Isn't it too good to be true? Won't it encourage me to sin more? I am glad you asked.

This is probably the biggest fear of the person afflicted by legalism: "Won't it cause me to excuse my sin? Won't it cause me to live in lawlessness? Won't it cause me to sin more?" Here is the answer: no. The point is, you repented from your sins didn't you? Haven't you experienced a change of heart? It is so important for us to understand that righteousness is a condition of the heart just like sin is a condition of the heart. You have experienced a change of heart, and you have received a new nature. The old is gone, the Bible says, and the new has come.[2] And your new nature hates sin and cannot go on sinning.[3] Ezekiel 36:26–27 describes this change in us: "A new heart will I give you and a new spirit will I put within you, and I will take away the stony heart out of your flesh and give you a heart of flesh. And I will put my Spirit

---

[1] Acts 16:28–31.
[2] See 1 Corinthians 5:17.
[3] See 1 John 3:9.

within you and cause you to walk in My statutes, and you shall heed My ordinances and do them."

Not only have we received a new nature, but the Spirit Himself will cause us to walk in His ways, according to the Scriptures. The Father who watches over our souls is the keeper of our souls.[4] So if there is something that we do that is wrong, He will make it known to us so we can repent and change our ways. Furthermore, when we receive such a gift for free, it causes us to love Him with our whole hearts; and again Jesus said that whoever really loves Him will obey Him.[5] And remember that because you have placed your faith in Christ, He is freed to show you mercy when you fall short. We cannot draw the same conclusion for someone under the law for we have learned that there is no room for mercy there.

About four years after my original cry to God, "What is wrong with me?" my youngest son Jonathan told me, "I love you because you are nice to me." I believe he was seven years old at the time.

I responded something like, "No, you love me because I am your mother!"

To which he answered back, "No. I love you because you are nice to me."

Now, believe me, I am far from being perfect, but I must have been really nice to him that day for him to speak these words. Likewise, we love God because He was nice to us; He died to set us free. We love Him because He first loved us.[6] And what should be our automatic response to such love? It is to love Him in return and to totally devote our lives to

---

[4] See Psalm 121:5.
[5] See John 14:15, 23.
[6] See 1 John 4:19.

Him.[7] Why? Because He devoted His life to us first. *This* is the simplicity that is in Christ of which 2 Corinthians 11:3 talks about: a wholehearted devotion to Christ as a direct, natural response to His love for us.

If you are hungry and thirsty for God, if you genuinely want salvation, you can have it through faith in Jesus Christ for free. That's it? You may ask. According to Isaiah 55:1, that is it, yes. "Wait and listen, everyone who is thirsty! Come to the waters; and he who has no money, come, buy and eat! Yes, come, buy [priceless, spiritual] wine and milk without money and without price [simply for the self-surrender that accepts the blessing]." Therefore, go ahead! Surrender and receive it!

What happens after we are saved? Answering this question is where the confusion can really set in. We receive our free gift of salvation without any works of our own, simply by faith in Christ the Lord, but what's next? Well here is the answer to every dilemma on this matter: The same way that we were saved is the same way that we ought to live—by faith. If it is in working for Him, our work can only be done through trusting Him to enable us, to provide for us, to help us, and to guide us. See what was discovered as Jesus' answer to the question of how we are to work the works of God? He responded, "That you believe in the One Whom He has sent."[8] If it is in changing us and sanctifying us, this can only happen as we earnestly trust His Holy Spirit to do it in us and by cooperating with Him by His grace to live increasingly holier lives as discussed earlier.[9] Everything is done by faith.

---

[7] See 2 Corinthians 11:3 AMPC.
[8] See John 6:28–29.
[9] See Galatians 3:3.

Such faith is provided to us and enabled by God.[10] It is where we choose to trust Him, a choice that is made by His grace.[11] Where is boasting then? It is excluded. By what law? The law of works? No, but by the law of faith. Anything done without faith, anything done in the flesh, anything done without dependence upon Him, is sin the Bible says, and is not pleasing to God.[12] Consequently, we are led by the Spirit of God moment by moment, as every child of God needs to be.[13] Jesus is our life.[14] This is why we need to feed on Him by spending time with Him regularly or we will grow weak.[15] Jesus is the vine and we are the branches.[16] There, God becomes our all in all and we enter into the rest of God because we depend on Him for everything.[17]

> For no matter how many promises God has made, they are "Yes" in Christ. And so through him the "Amen" is spoken by us to the glory of God. Now it is God who makes both us and you stand firm in Christ. He anointed us, set his seal of ownership on us, and put his Spirit in our hearts as a deposit, guaranteeing what is to come.
>
> —2 Corinthians 1:20–22 NIV

---

[10] See Romans 12:3; Matthew 16:17.
[11] See Ephesians 2:8.
[12] See Romans 14:23; Hebrews 11:6.
[13] See Romans 8:14.
[14] See Colossians 3:4.
[15] See John 6:57.
[16] See John 15:5.
[17] See Ephesians 4:6; Hebrews 4:3.

Recreated Unto Good Works

For we are God's [own] handiwork (His work-manship), recreated in Christ Jesus, [born anew] that we may do those good works which God predestined (planned beforehand) for us [taking paths which He prepared ahead of time], that we should walk in them [living the good life which He prearranged and made ready for us to live].

—Ephesians 2:10

We have learned that the Bible refers to two kinds of works: works that require no faith (works of the flesh) and works that originate from faith.[18] One kind relies on the flesh to attain righteousness, the other relies on the Holy Spirit. One is performed in order to be made right with God, the other is carried out because we have been made right with God already. One relies on dos and don'ts, the other relies on "done." One is performed out of obligation, the other is performed out of love. One is done in frustration, the other is done at rest. One attempts to do a work from the outside, the other does a work from the inside out. One fosters pride, the other fosters humility. One draws glory to self, the other brings glory to God.

Hebrews 9:14 says, "How much more surely shall the blood of Christ, Who by virtue of [His] eternal Spirit [His own preexistent divine personality] has offered Himself as an un-blemished sacrifice to God, purify our consciences from dead

---

[18] See Galatians 3:12; James 2:17.

works and lifeless observances to serve the [ever] living God?"

We no longer need to serve Him out of a sense of obligation. Instead, we have been recreated to serve Him because we *want* to. It is a deep-seated desire within every child of God to fulfill the will of God for their life; we want to finish our course; we want to complete our destiny. As born-again believers, we serve Him first and foremost because we love Him. As such, we long to please Him and to hear Him say, "Well done, you upright (honorable, admirable) and faithful servant! You have been faithful and trustworthy over a little; I will put you in charge of much. Enter into and share the joy (the delight, the blessedness) which your master enjoys."[19]

We are literally wired by the Holy Spirit in us to want to do the work of God. We pray for God to use us. We pray to know His will. Didn't Jesus say that it was His very food to do the will of His Father?[20] I am not saying that we feel up to the task, however, nor am I saying that we like every task. No, quite the contrary. As a matter of fact, what God calls us to do will normally be something for which we feel completely inadequate. And this is why we must do it in faith, trusting Him and His Word that whatever He calls us to do, He has also equipped us and anointed us for it.[21] We need to depend on Him each step of the way, because the deeper we go in Him, the more we realize how helpless we are without Him and that apart from Him we can do nothing indeed.

God made sure to highlight in His Word that He calls the weak and the foolish things of this world to confound the

---

[19] See Matthew 25:23.
[20] See John 4:34.
[21] See Hebrews 13:21.

wise.[22] It is a very humbling thing to know that He chose us because we were weak and foolish! In Isaiah we see that we were poor and afflicted, brokenhearted, captive, and blind. Then the Lord came on the scene, and, as the Anointed One, saved us, gave us His righteousness as a free gift, made us brand new, and then began a work in us.

> The Spirit of the Lord God is upon me, because the Lord has anointed and qualified me to preach the Gospel of good tidings to the meek, the poor, and afflicted; He has sent me to bind up and heal the brokenhearted, to proclaim liberty to the [physical and spiritual] captives and the opening of the prison and of the eyes to those who are bound, To proclaim the acceptable year of the Lord [the year of His favor] and the day of vengeance of our God, to comfort all who mourn, To grant [consolation and joy] to those who mourn in Zion—to give them an ornament (a garland or diadem) of beauty instead of ashes, the oil of joy instead of mourning, the garment [expressive] of praise instead of a heavy, burdened, and failing spirit—that they may be called oaks of righteousness [lofty, strong, and magnificent, distinguished for uprightness, justice, and right standing with God], the planting of the Lord, that He may be glorified.[23]

Through this work of the Lord, He is healing us, molding us, and shaping us into His image from glory to glory that

---

[22] See 1 Corinthians 1:27 KJV.
[23] Isaiah 61:1–3.

we may be called oaks of righteousness, lofty, strong and magnificent, distinguished for uprightness, just, in right standing with God, and the planting of the Lord, that He may be glorified. And this is entirely His doing. He is the Potter and we are the clay.[24] This process takes time; it takes many hours and a lot of hard work—not a work of the flesh, but a work quickened and energized by the Holy Spirit within. Grace doesn't exclude hard work, but the work that we do stems from actively believing God and depending on Him. It is a place where we earnestly put our hope in His Word and His promises, which causes us to direct our lives and to make choices accordingly.

Do you remember that "prophetess" Paul and I met at the convenience store? She thought her calling was to warn women not to wear pants. This was a work she was imposing on God's children in order to make them right with God. But to be a child of God is to be led by the Holy Spirit. It is to make decisions based on His finished work at the cross, knowing that by His work we have already been made right with Him. Let the Holy Spirit guide you even as to how to dress. He is interested in everything that concerns you. Let us follow His leading, and we are sure not to go wrong. We are not bound to a dress code, but we have been set free to follow the leadership of the Holy Spirit. Always make sure to study the whole counsel of the Word of God. Moreover, there are Bible verses that are better understood within the context of the times in which they were written. Finally, understand that the interpretation of every Scripture must be built on the solid foundation of God's grace and finished work at the cross.

---

[24] See Jeremiah 18:6.

Again, look at Jesus' response when people asked Him about the works of God. "They then said, What are we to do, that we may [habitually] be working the works of God? [What are we to do to carry out what God requires?] Jesus replied, This is the work (service) that God asks of you: that you believe in the One Whom He has sent [that you cleave to, trust, rely on, and have faith in His Messenger]."[25]

The work that God has called us to do is to believe in Jesus. Out of that faith, deeds of obedience and service will naturally spring forth. James puts it this way: "What is the use (profit), my brethren, for anyone to profess to have faith if he has no [good] works [to show for it]? Can [such] faith save [his soul]? . . . So also faith, if it does not have works (deeds and actions of obedience to back it up), by itself is destitute of power (inoperative, dead)."[26] We have to be so careful in the way that we interpret this Scripture. It does not say that we must do works to save ourselves or to make ourselves acceptable to God. It does not say that we need to perform apart from faith. No, what James is saying here is that when we have a genuine faith, a saving faith, works will naturally flow out of that faith.

Really, only such works, which originate from our new nature within, the one that has been recreated unto good works, are acceptable to God. Any works that spring forth out of any other source will be rejected and burned up on that glorious day.[27] Only works done out of a pure heart, a clear conscience, and a sincere faith are acceptable to God.[28] Any

---

[25] John 6:28–29.
[26] James 2:14, 17.
[27] See 1 Corinthians 3:15.
[28] See 1 Timothy 1:5.

other works are what the Bible calls dead works as we already read in Hebrews 9:14.

As mentioned previously, it takes humility to receive a gift we do not deserve. I am amazed at how reluctant people are to receive just a free coffee or a free tea from me. If I get them something free, they insist that the next time it will be their turn to buy! Sometimes I just want to bless them without expecting anything in return, but I have come to realize that it is very hard for people to just receive without earning it or paying for it in some way or fashion. Oh, the wisdom of God in His plan of redemption, for only a free gift can set us free from pride, selfishness, and self-centeredness. Only a free gift can purge our conscience from dead works and set us free to serve the living God and can thus purify our motives.

> Let's return to Isaiah 61 and see what comes next. And they shall rebuild the ancient ruins; they shall raise up the former desolations and renew the ruined cities, the devastations of many generations. Aliens shall stand [ready] and feed your flocks, and foreigners shall be your plowmen and your vinedressers. But you shall be called the priests of the Lord; people will speak of you as the ministers of our God. You shall eat the wealth of the nations, and the glory [once that of your captors] shall be yours. Instead of your [former] shame you shall have a twofold recompense; instead of dishonor and reproach [your people] shall rejoice in their portion. Therefore in their land they shall possess double

241

[what they had forfeited]; everlasting joy shall be theirs.[29]

Alleluia! Did you read that? In this chapter in Isaiah, we are told that God first does a work in us and then, in turn, our destiny consists of rebuilding the ancient ruins, raising up the former desolations, and renewing ruined cities and the devastation of many generations. This is what you and I have been called to do. Out of our pain will come the unfolding of our destiny through God's saving us and restoring us to wholeness in Him.

According to Romans 12:2, once we are transformed, we will prove for ourselves the good and acceptable and perfect will of God for our lives. In the days I was still taking singing lessons, my teacher said to me "Don't worry about the power; the power is there within you. As you build your instrument, the power will come out." However, when she spoke to me, it strongly resonated with my spirit, and I sensed that God was speaking to me concerning spiritual matters through her lips. In other words, as we are being built, as we are being transformed from the inside out, the power of God will be released more and more to flow out of our lives as hindrances are being removed.

Now you may ask, who is working then? Well, for one thing, when you stop working, God starts. But He will not start until you stop. But, you may say, doesn't the Bible say to work out our own salvation with fear and trembling? I am glad you asked. Let's read the Scripture you are talking about together.

---

[29] Isaiah 61:4–7.

Therefore, my dear ones, as you have always obeyed [my suggestions], so now, not only [with the enthusiasm you would show] in my presence but much more because I am absent, *work out* (cultivate, carry out to the goal, and fully complete) your own salvation with reverence and awe and trembling (self-distrust, with serious caution, tenderness of conscience, watchfulness against temptation, timidly shrinking from whatever might offend God and discredit the name of Christ). [*Not in your own strength*] for *it is God* Who is all the while effectually at *work in you* [energizing and creating in you the power and desire], both to will and to work for His good pleasure and satisfaction and delight.[30]

I love how Derek Prince puts it in his book *By Grace Alone*, where he says that as God works *in*, we work *out*.[31] Basically, we can only work *out* what God first works *in*. Hence, it is no longer done in our own strength, but instead we receive the grace that God first works in us both to will and to do of His good pleasure. I believe it was two to three years after I was born again, God gave me a dream. In the dream I saw a woman evangelist. Then, I saw her shirt being taken off of her. There was nothing inappropriate; her upper body was made blurry in appearance. All I saw was the blurry picture of her skin. I could see her side being pressed and molded as with invisible hands. God was showing me that He is the one molding and shaping our hearts. He also revealed that it takes

---

[30] Philippians 2:12–13, emphasis added.
[31] Prince, *By Grace Alone*, 113.

many hours and a lot of hard work. We do need to cooperate with Him as He transforms us within; and we do that by believing that He is working in us even when we do not see immediate results and by yielding to His molding. We also cooperate by studying His Word and by praying. That way, our mind is renewed. This represents the time and the effort that we put in. Then, as He does the work in us, we begin to work out what He is doing inwardly.

Now, the best part. Our reward. You may be shocked when I say to you that our present reward for following Christ is holiness. If you don't believe me, read the following Scripture: "But now since you have been set free from sin and have become the slaves of God, you have your present reward in holiness and its end is eternal life."[32] Our recompense is to be partakers of His holiness. What He has, He wants us to have also and to enjoy. He withholds nothing from us and that also goes for His very nature, the essence of who He is. The Bible says in 2 Peter 1:4 that we have become partakers of His divine nature. Holiness is not a punishment, or a heavy burden. Instead, it is the very essence and the very nature of who God is. The Devil has twisted this truth and made us see holiness as a burden instead of a promise.

The apostle Paul wrote in his letter to the Christians in Rome: "But to one who, not working [by the Law], trusts (believes fully) in Him Who justifies the ungodly, his faith is credited to him as righteousness (the standing acceptable to God)."[33] We see clearly here that one can never earn a right standing with God on the merit of works. Instead, we are told that we must humbly receive our right standing with God by

---

[32] Romans 6:22.
[33] Romans 4:5.

faith alone; and a sign that we have received our right standing with God by faith alone will be the deeds of obedience, or in other words, the works, that follow.

Working Faithfully

> Even so it is that Christ, having been offered to take upon Himself and bear as a burden the sins of many once and once for all, will appear a second time, not to carry any burden of sin nor to deal with sin, but to bring to full salvation those who are [eagerly, constantly, and patiently] waiting for and expecting Him.
>
> —Hebrews 9:28

My husband had a dream a while back. In the dream, the rapture had just happened. As he looked around, he saw work boots all over the ground but no one in the boots. The boot heals were still standing upward. This suggested that the speed with which the people had been taken up and out of their boots was really fast, like as fast as the twinkling of an eye.[34] The work boots suggested that Jesus was coming back for a people who were busy working faithfully for Him.

Christ is coming back for those who are eagerly, constantly, and patiently waiting for and expecting Him. A sign that someone is expecting his master to return is that he remains sober and alert and busies himself doing his master's will. This analogy is also found in the parable of the faithful steward.[35] God is not looking for perfection, or else none of us

---

[34] See 1 Corinthians 15:52.
[35] See Luke 12:42–48.

would have any chance of ever making it in. As a matter of fact, the Bible says we are falling short of the glory of God.[36] However, He does want to see us pressing forward toward the mark of perfection and of the high calling in Christ Jesus when He returns. He wants to see us faithfully using the gift(s) and the talent(s) that He has given us for the advancing of His kingdom. I believe we will be asked to give an account of what we did with our free gift of salvation the day we stand before Him. He wants to see us following the leadership of the Holy Spirit and walking in obedience to His voice when He comes back. In other words, He desires faithfulness.

I want to reiterate that how we see God is very important. Seeing God through the sterile lenses of legalism not only will wound our soul and chain our spirit but will hinder, if not completely stop, all progress in our lives. Listen closely to what Jesus said in the following Scriptures:

> For it is like a man who was about to take a long journey, and he called his servants together and entrusted them with his property. To one he gave five talents [probably about $5,000], to another two, to another one—to each in proportion to his own personal ability. Then he departed and left the country.... He who had received one talent also came forward, saying, Master, I knew you to be a harsh and hard man, reaping where you did not sow, and gathering where you had not winnowed [the grain]. So I was afraid, and I went and hid your talent in the ground. Here you have what is your own. But

---

his master answered him, You wicked and lazy and idle servant! Did you indeed know that I reap where I have not sowed and gather [grain] where I have not winnowed? Then you should have invested my money with the bankers, and at my coming I would have received what was my own with interest. So take the talent away from him and give it to the one who has the ten talents. For to everyone who has will more be given, and he will be furnished richly so that he will have an abundance; but from the one who does not have, even what he does have will be taken away. And throw the good-for-nothing servant into the outer darkness; there will be weeping and grinding of teeth.[37]

This account indicates that the view of a harsh and hard master, the way that the third servant saw his Lord, paralyzed him from bearing any fruit. Note that this was not a good excuse in the eyes of Christ. We can see from this story that it will make it difficult for you and me to bear good and lasting fruit on a consistent basis for the kingdom of God if our view of God is distorted or unbalanced. We need to know the severity of the Lord, but we must also know the goodness and the gentleness of our Lord. This servant's view of God terrified the man, and all he could do for fear of displeasing the master was nothing. I personally believe the servant represents someone under the grip of legalism. But even if that is not the case, someone who has an unbalanced view of God, putting way more weight on His severity without bringing in

---

[37] Matthew 25:14–15, 24–30.

the much needed complement of His love, will fear God with a tormenting type of fear. Such fear is unhealthy and will interrupt all genuine growth in the life of the believer. Any appearance of growth will be only something happening on the surface, but there will not be a real and transforming work of the heart. The antidote for such fear is given to us in 1 John 4:18, and it is love.

In the early days of my battle against legalism, God showed me that not only was I in spiritual adultery but I was taking the control and placing myself as the one in authority over my life when I should have humbled myself and let God be the ruler. I was a backup singer at our church at the time. After this revelation, there was no way I could just keep leading God's people in worship when I was in such condition! Yes, I had repented, meaning I had chosen to turn around; but obviously I had major problems still so, certainly, I couldn't do ministry, especially not worship, of all ministries. I needed to stop being part of the worship team for a while so I could get my act together first. After all, how could I possibly be in a position to lead God's people in worship if I struggled with such gross sin? So that morning I set myself to speak to the senior pastor of our church and to let him know that I would step down from the worship ministry for a while. He was shocked to say the least. You see, he was ready to promote me from being a backup singer to becoming a worship leader. As a result, I agreed with him that I would give it a day (that day) to see if something was going to happen that would convince me to change my mind and to remain on the team.

That day, a guest speaker was ministering at our church. What he preached really ministered to me. That night (we have services on Sunday morning and on Sunday night), to my surprise, the Lord touched me, and I was able to worship the Lord in spirit and in truth and experienced some sort of deliverance. At least I felt some freedom, such that I had not experienced in quite a while until then. That night, I believe the Lord rid me of demonic spirits that oppressed me. I was far from being completely recovered, and I still had a huge and long battle ahead of me; but I knew then that God wanted me to continue in the ministry even though it would take me a long time to get well again. I therefore made the decision to remain on the worship team, by faith. Based on my experience and on Jesus' parable, it is important we remain faithful to use the gifts that the Lord has given us even during our recovery process. I am not saying that someone who commits willful sin should continue in ministry, but I am suggesting that if you have repented, meaning you have decided to turn around and cooperate with God for complete recovery, then you need to stay in the ministry by faith.

The Law of Liberty

So speak and so act as [people should] who are to be judged under the law of liberty [the moral instruction given by Christ, especially about love].

—James 2:12

"The battle is over. Satan's been defeated. He's been crushed like a bug under the feet of Jesus. When Jesus cried 'it is finished' it was over. He won the victory for you that day."[38] Again, because of the one single offering of Christ on the cross, we, as children of God, have received a new heart and a new nature. We have been made partakers of God's divine nature. As people who have already been made right, we are enabled to live righteously. Because we are right with God, we are empowered to behave right. As God works in us, we work out—all by the grace of God through exercising our faith in His work on the cross. The law of liberty is it. It consists of being faithful in using and manifesting what God has already worked in us. It is living at the level of conduct that God has given us. It is being empowered by the Holy Spirit within to do good works. As God provides divine appointments and divine opportunities to let our light shine, we are enabled to love one another by relying on His Holy Spirit. The Bible says that it is the love of Christ that compels us.[39] He never requires us to give away something that He hasn't first given us. That being said, we are called only to live at the level of conduct that we have received. We mess up, we miss opportunities, we fail, and we fall every so often. But God is pleased with the heart that is genuine and that desires growth, someone who desires to obey Him and to live a life of victory. Someone who hungers and thirsts for righteousness is bound to make progress. Someone who hungers and thirsts for holiness is bound to change. Certainly His yoke is easy and His burden is light.

Let us remember that our very foundation, the very first layer of our building, need always be the grace of God. Then we can safely add the reverential fear of the Lord on top of the layer of grace. But we cannot change this order and re-

[38] "The Battle Is Over," (Paul Kaczmarek).
[39] See 2 Corinthians 5:14 AMP.

main victorious. We are first accepted through our faith in Christ, then we are enabled to reverentially fear the Lord with a healthy fear. If the order is changed, we will become afraid of God. Only the grace of God can enable us to fear God properly.

The Bible says in Proverbs 9:10, "The reverent and worshipful fear of the Lord is the beginning (the chief and choice part) of Wisdom, and the knowledge of the Holy One is insight and understanding." We fear Him because we know from the Word of God that He is no respecter of persons and that, just like the Scriptures say, God is not mocked; we will reap what we sow.[40] This Scripture along with the discussion we had in chapter 2 indicates that if we habitually sow mercy, we will reap mercy. If we habitually sow judgment and criticism, we will reap judgment and criticism. "For to him who has shown no mercy the judgment [will be] merciless, but mercy [full of glad confidence] exults victoriously over judgment."[41] The Bible further says that only if we forgive our offenders their offence, will we be forgiven our offences by the Father.[42] God expects us to forgive our offender because we were forgiven by Him first. Again, we cannot give anything we don't have. Because we have forgiveness, He is asking us to forgive as a natural result.

Remember the section on understanding repentance and how I was so scared of the Scriptures that say that unless we forgive others we will not be forgiven?[43] Remember how God helped eliminate the undue fear associated with these

---

[40] See Acts 10:34; Galatians 6:7.
[41] James 2:13.
[42] See Mark 11:26.
[43] See the section "Understanding Repentance" in chapter 4.

Scriptures? He showed me that what He is looking for is a genuine decision to forgive. It was okay if the feelings would catch up later. My genuine repentance, that is my sincere decision to forgive causing me to begin to walk in the opposite direction, and my change of mind toward unforgiveness and toward the person who offended me, was acceptable even if my feelings had not quite caught up yet. Why? Because repentance will always yield fruit that will begin a work with God to change my feelings toward the person. All the while, I am okay.

However, if we persist in choosing justice and if we refuse to extend forgiveness, justice and unforgiveness is what the Bible says we will reap; and we all know that should God deal with us according to what we deserve, we are in *big* trouble. So in this life, we have control over how the judgment day will go. We can choose to depend on God to do the right thing here on earth through the knowledge that we have been made right already by grace through faith and be thus empowered to extend love and mercy as a result. Or we can consistently persist in withholding mercy. The choice is ours. In 1 John 4:17 it says that if we walk in love here on this earth as a response to His love, we will have confidence and boldness before God.

I remember an incident which I believe took place while I was still recovering from legalism. Paul, the kids, and I were all in the car, the kids were arguing about something. I don't remember the details, but I remember the essence of the lesson. Jonathan had done something, and Aaron was upset and demanded justice. He wanted Jonathan to pay for his action. I think he may even have suggested the way that Jonathan should be punished. However, it was not long after that

Aaron did the *exact* same thing Jonathan had just done! This is
when I either told Aaron or thought to myself that the punishment he saw fit for Jonathan would, or at least should, be
the same punishment that he was going to undergo. I was
amazed at what had just happened, because I knew that a
great spiritual lesson was being taught there.

There lies the danger in becoming judgmental and critical toward others. And we know what Jesus thinks of such
practices. Jesus rebuked those who were busy judging others
yet not being mindful of their own sin.[44] We have to be so
careful when we start acting like a judge toward other people.
I have such reverential fear in that area. We do not want to
judge anybody else for anything they do. Again, didn't the
apostle Paul say in Romans 14:4, "Who are you to pass judgment on and censure another's household servant? It is before
his own master that he stands or falls. And he shall stand and
be upheld, for the Master (the Lord) is mighty to support him
and make him stand"?

We learn from 2 Peter 1 that love does not just auto-
matically happen, but that we need to make a continuous effort if we want to grow in love. We need to diligently work
with God toward the mark of perfection. "For this very reason, applying your diligence [to the divine promises, make
every effort] in [exercising] your faith to, develop moral excellence, and in moral excellence, knowledge (insight, understanding), and in your knowledge, self-control, and in your
self-control, steadfastness, and in your steadfastness, godliness, and in your godliness, brotherly affection, and in your
brotherly affection, [develop Christian] love [that is, learn to

[44] See Matthew 7:3.

unselfishly seek the best for others and to do things for their benefit]."[45]

From this Scripture we see that we are called to grow and to mature from glory to glory. Let us therefore ask God to help us make progress daily as we exercise our faith toward the mark of perfection knowing that all the while we are accepted in the beloved even though we have not arrived yet.[46] Let us, by God's grace, conduct our lives as people who are to be judged under the law of liberty.

> For you, brethren, were [indeed] called to freedom; only [do not let your] freedom be an incentive to your flesh and an opportunity or excuse [for selfishness], but through love you should serve one another.
>
> —Galatians 5:13

Press On and Never Give Up!

> I do not consider, brethren, that I have captured and made it my own [yet]; but one thing I do [it is my one aspiration]: forgetting what lies behind and straining forward to what lies ahead, I press on toward the goal to win the [supreme and heavenly] prize to which God in Christ Jesus is calling us upward.
>
> —Philippians 3:13–14

---

[45] 2 Peter 1:5–7 AMP.
[46] See Ephesians 1:6; Philippians 3:13.

Serving God

A friend of mine shared with me a dream that God gave her. In the dream, she started walking up a spiral staircase in an old castle. The stairway reached to heaven. When she looked up, she saw clear blue sky. When she looked down, she saw thick, bottomless darkness. She heard a voice speak to her: "The road to heaven is like climbing these narrow stairs. If you don't keep climbing up, you will fall down."

See how the apostle Paul puts it in Philippians 3:13–14. We see clearly that he refused to focus on the past, on what was behind him, on what was below him. He chose to forget the past. He also refused to stay stagnant. Instead he pressed on toward the goal to win the prize for which Christ had called him upward. We need to do the same. This doesn't mean we forget what the Lord has done for us in the past. The Bible is clear that we are to remember all of the things the Lord has done for us because they are a source of encouragement to us and a reason to praise and to glorify Him.[47] However, we are to forget everything that will not benefit us and what will distract us from our course, like our mistakes or others' mistakes for instance.

We also read something along these same lines in Hebrews 12:2 AMP: "[looking away from all that will distract us and] focusing our eyes on Jesus, who is the Author and Perfecter of faith [the first incentive for our belief and the One who brings our faith to maturity], who for the joy [of accomplishing the goal] set before Him endured the cross, disregarding the shame, and sat down at the right hand of the throne of God [revealing His deity, His authority, and the completion of His work]."

---

[47] See Deuteronomy 8:2; Psalm 105:5–6.

The higher we want to go, the deeper our foundation needs to be. Pray regularly, ask God for help, and be very attentive to His voice daily. He will speak to you and lead you as you trust Him to do so. Remember to make the Word a priority in your life. As you keep choosing the truth, your feelings will follow. *Press on!*

> So trust in the Lord (commit yourself to Him, lean on Him, hope confidently in Him) forever; for the Lord God is an everlasting Rock [the Rock of Ages].
>
> —Isaiah 26:4

I just love what Lisa Bevere says in her book *Out of Control and Loving It!*: "Fear had so twisted and perverted their spiritual perception of God that the Israelites imagined God had tricked them. They believed He had delivered them from Egyptian oppression in order to turn them over to be slaughtered by the heathen nations of Canaan."[48] O that we may be ministered to by the fact that Christ has not come to condemn us, but that He has come so that through Him we may be saved![49] And if, while we were God's enemies, we were reconciled to Him through the death of His Son, how much more, having been reconciled, shall we be saved through His life?[50] Let us therefore be of the same spirit as Joshua and Caleb who never doubted God's heart and ability to deliver, and let us take courage and know that it is only a

---

[48] Lisa Bevere, *Out of Control and Loving It! Giving God Complete Control of Your Life* (Lake Mary, Fla.: Charisma House, 2006), 105.
[49] See John 3:17.
[50] See Romans 5:10 NIV.

matter of time until full deliverance comes.[51] For we know that weeping may endure for a night but joy comes in the morning.[52] I like what Joyce Meyer says: "We need to outlast the Devil." Let us therefore submit ourselves to God, resist the Devil, and he will flee from us.[53]

As you read through the pages of this book, you may have quickly come to realize that we are in a battle. I really had to fight for my freedom and you may now realize that you may have to fight for yours also. However, we know He is well able to see us through to the finish line, and we can take comfort in the fact that Jesus promised never to leave us nor forsake us.[54] We are also encouraged by the Scripture that says that even though a righteous man falls seven times, he will get back up again.[55] No matter how long it takes, no matter how many times we fall, let us not be weary in well doing for we will reap in due season if we faint not. [56] Let us be wise and therefore determined to be free. It takes what I call holy determination, but I can guarantee you that if you will really hook up with God and work with Him to get free from this mess, you will be free. It may take some time and a lot of hard work, work that springs from faith, but if you will not give up, it is only a matter of time until you are free. But you *must* determine never to give up and to always get back up again should you fall along the way. Your attitude need be: "I will not quit even if I have to die pressing on." You must *choose*, as far as you are concerned, that from glory to glory you will be

---

[51] See Numbers 13:30; Numbers 14:24, 30.
[52] See Psalm 30:5.
[53] See James 4:7.
[54] See Matthew 28:20.
[55] See Proverbs 24:16.
[56] See Galatians 6:9 KJV.

restored. God will move heaven and earth for you if you will adopt such an attitude.

Please note who is telling you this! Remember, I reached a point where I could hardly sleep. I wondered how much longer my body and mind could bear such intense mental torture, but when I cried out to God with my whole heart, even though I was in the depth of my sin, He quickly answered and ultimately brought deliverance.

If we want to make progress in the Lord, we need to make progress on purpose. In order to make progress, we need to desire it, and we need to go after it with all of our hearts. We need to want all of the obstacles out of the way. What we need to do is tackle one obstacle at a time. So focus on one with God until it is dealt with then move on to the next and to the next and to the next until you really enjoy the life that Christ died to give you. Now when I say "focus on one," I do not mean to keep thinking about your sin and how you need to stop it somehow. This is the law and it will only strengthen the sin and delay victory over it. What I mean is repent from your sin, commit the obstacle to God in prayer, trust Him to deliver you and focus on Jesus and His finished work where it concerns this sin. As you do that, deliverance will come, your mind will be renewed and you will become more and more like Jesus in this area until this shortcoming is completely gone.

I encourage you to look at your priorities and perhaps reestablish them. The Bible invites us to seek first the kingdom of God and His righteousness and all of these other things will be given to us.[57] As you choose to put God first

---

[57] See Matthew 6:33.

and seek Him in the areas where you know there are hindrances, strongholds, and obstacles to overcome, He will see you through. As you pray and study the Word in those areas of need, as you read anointed Christian books related to your need, as you wait on Him and expect Him to intervene in those areas, and as you depend on Him constantly, He will deliver you. I hope that makes sense to you. This is my story, and I know that God is faithful. He will complete that which He began in us. Remember Proverbs 3:6, which promises that as we acknowledge Him in all of our ways He will direct our paths. Remember 1 Peter 5:7, which tells us to cast the whole of our care on Him for He cares for us.

As soon as you sincerely repent of legalism, God is right there with you to help you back on your feet; and this is what He is saying to us: "Fear not, for I am with you."[58] He promised in His Word that when we are in Christ, when we trust Him, He *always* causes us to triumph.[59] Through it all, the Lord is with you, and He will see you through. Hang on to the truth. He did say that He will uphold us with His righteous right hand and that even though we may fall He is able to make us stand.[60] Therefore, even if you fall, let your faith keep standing and see the deliverance of the Lord. He said, "Return to the stronghold [of security and prosperity], you prisoners of hope; even today do I declare that I will restore double your former prosperity to you."[61] Hold on to His promise!

---

[58] See Isaiah 41:10.
[59] See 2 Corinthians 2:14.
[60] See Isaiah 41:10; Romans 14:4.
[61] Zechariah 9:12.

Remember my singing lessons? Nothing was working, or at least not on a consistent basis, and not until close to the very end. I went through all the lessons, and I still didn't feel like I had a hold on it quite yet. Only, not long before the final concert, it all finally started to come together, at the very end! What if I had given up? The only thing that kept me going was that God had spoken very clearly that He called me to sing. He is the one who told me to take those singing lessons. Many times I wanted to give up so badly. I remember especially one time when I was standing in my living room, I really almost gave up. At that moment, I had to remind myself that if I gave up, that meant that I also had to give up on the entire call; because just like God had called me to sing, God had also called me to preach. If I didn't believe in the one, then the other couldn't be true either. So I had to persevere or I would lose everything I had believed, my very purpose on the earth! So I persevered and finally got a breakthrough. I remember one day in the car, I was trying to sing and struggled. But then something happened that day, because I said, "This belongs to me! I will sing! And I sang in spite of my fears." You see, I feared that if I allowed power to come out, I would somehow hurt my voice; and this fear hindered me from making progress.

When we fear that moving forward will hurt us, it keeps us from making any progress. So no longer allow fear to keep you from receiving everything that Jesus died to give you. You can trust Jesus. Get some holy anger about yourself and boldly take what belongs to you in Jesus' name. I am sharing this with you because I remember another day in the car again. That day, however, was different, for I was finally experiencing victory! I could sing with much more ease; and in gladness I thanked the Lord. However, when I thanked Him, it was as though I heard Him respond: "No, thank *you* for not giving up."

If you are at all like I was, you may be starting to see the truth and even believe the truth, but you may be afraid to walk in it. Maybe you are afraid of what your legalistic friends will say if you believe the gospel message, if you believe in the grace of God. You may be concerned they will accuse you of trying to excuse sin. You may be concerned that your church will call you a heretic. You may fear opposition. You may be afraid to be labelled as one who condones lawlessness. However, we know now that such accusations are erroneous, for we have learned that the grace of God teaches us to say no to ungodliness.[62] The grace of God does not condone sin at all, but instead the grace of God sets us free from both the guilt and the power of sin. Through the Holy Spirit we are empowered to live a holy life as we are changed from glory to glory. Again, grace cleanses us from dead works so that we are free to serve the living God with pure motives.

You may be fearful to step into what you know to be true and sound doctrine. I too went through a similar struggle. I wondered what in the world was wrong with me. I thought, *Don't I know the truth by now?* But I still felt fearful and anxious. I finally believed the truth about God's grace, but why was I still experiencing anxiety? Even though I knew the truth, I had a hard time committing to it and walking in it. Was legalism still my problem after all that God had revealed to me?

---

[62] See Romans 8:28.

In God's goodness and mercy, He gave me a dream to answer my question. I do not remember much of the dream anymore, but I remember this one sentence: "Your problem is not legalism but leadership." God showed me that I knew the truth, but that I needed to exercise leadership to dare to start living in it even if it meant that I had to be the only one in my circle of church friends to do so. I needed leadership. And by daring to lead, others would follow and the truth would prevail. From that day, I asked the Lord to help me develop and exercise leadership and dare to believe the truth for myself, to walk in it, and to proclaim it whether alone or not. And He did help me. As I began to take steps of faith and to commit to the truth, God saw me through.

Therefore, let us not be ashamed of the gospel of Christ "for it is the power of God for salvation [from His wrath and punishment] to everyone who believes [in Christ as Savior], to the Jew first and also to the Greek."[63]

Still in the days I was taking singing lessons, my teacher said to me "Don't worry, the day will come when everything will come together." Again, when she spoke these words, I knew the Lord was speaking to me concerning spiritual matters. He was reassuring me that the day would come when all of the confusion caused by legalism would be gone and all the pieces of the puzzle would finally come together in harmony.

What is written in this book is definitely first and foremost for your benefit. However, it is useful for me as well; I need to continue to grow in the revelations that God has graciously given me, and this book is a great tool to help me

---

[63] See Romans 1:16 AMP.

with that. I ask the Lord to continue to deepen the revelations that He has given me on this topic from glory to glory for I am all too aware of the Devil's schemes.

Our progress will be tested. The Devil does not give up on us that easy. Don't despair, don't be discouraged, only trust God. The Devil will try you in your areas of struggle from different angles to try to gain entrance again. Don't get discouraged if you feel you are like a yo-yo for a while. Instead, rejoice that for every battle won, one more stronghold or lie has been destroyed, until every single one of them has been removed and all lies have been replaced with the truth.

I understood pretty quickly that it was going to be a fight, probably the fight of my life, but that with and through God, I was going to overcome. And you will too. Remember that it is only a matter of time, for victory is always ours when we put our faith in God. We need to only believe and trust Him. And so this is it. Walking by faith. Take courage, God loves you; and by His grace and mercy, this too shall pass. Roll up your sleeves, and make up your mind that with God on your side you will defeat that Goliath[64] no matter how hard it is or how long it takes. This is not an easy journey, but it is worth it. God has not lost a battle yet! Therefore, make Him your leader and your chief commander, choose to come under His authority and do what He says, and assured victory is yours in Jesus' name!

***

Psalm 116 AMP, Thanksgiving for Rescue from Death.

I love the LORD, because He hears [and continues to hear] My voice and my supplications (my

---

[64] See the story of David and Goliath in 1 Samuel 17.

pleas, my cries, my specific needs). Because He
has inclined His ear to me, Therefore I will call
on Him as long as I live. The cords and sorrows
of death encompassed me, And the terrors of
Sheol came upon me; I found distress and sor-
row. Then I called on the name of the LORD: "O
LORD, please save my life!" Gracious is the
LORD, and [consistently] righteous; Yes, our God
is compassionate. The LORD protects the simple
(childlike); I was brought low [humbled and
discouraged], and He saved me. Return to your
rest, O my soul, For the LORD has dealt bounti-
fully with you. For You have rescued my life
from death, My eyes from tears, And my feet
from stumbling and falling. I will walk [in submissive wonder] before the LORD In the land of
the living. I believed [and clung to my God]
when I said, "I am greatly afflicted." I said in my
alarm, "All men are liars." What will I give to
the LORD [in return] For all His benefits toward
me? [How can I repay Him for His precious
blessings?] I will lift up the cup of salvation And
call on the name of the LORD. I will pay my
vows to the LORD, Yes, in the presence of all His
people. Precious [and of great consequence] in
the sight of the LORD Is the death of His godly
ones [so He watches over them]. O LORD, truly I
am Your servant; I am Your servant, the son of
Your handmaid; You have unfastened my
chains. I will offer to You the sacrifice of thanksgiving, And will call on the name of the LORD. I

will pay my vows to the LORD, Yes, in the presence of all His people, In the courts of the LORD's house (temple) — In the midst of you, O Jerusalem. Praise the LORD! (Hallelujah!)

How to receive Christ as your Personal Lord and Savior

If obeying God always represents an effort and seems to be a constant struggle, it may be that you have religion but not salvation. When we are born again, we are given a new nature, we are given a new heart.[1] The Bible says that God works in us both to will and to do of His good pleasure.[2] The Bible declares that we have been given the gift of righteousness,[3] given by God free of charge. A healthy child of God longs earnestly for righteousness and has a strong desire to obey God and to do His will daily. It is that new nature that causes us to hunger for righteousness more and more in our inner man. You know the saying, "Like Father, like son." (Also, like Father, like daughter!) We certainly do not become perfect in our performance the moment the Holy Spirit comes to live in our hearts. Nevertheless, something changes drastically and we enter a journey where, step by step, we walk toward the goal of perfection. I am not talking about a lifeless and sterile aim for perfection. No, rather, I am talking about growing daily to become more like Jesus, full of grace and truth, where the love of God rules and reigns in our hearts.[4]

The Bible says in Romans 10:10: "For with the heart a person believes (adheres to, trusts in, and relies on Christ) and so is justified (declared righteous, acceptable to God), and with the mouth he confesses (declares openly and speaks out freely his faith) and confirms [his] salvation."

---

[1] See Ezekiel 36:26.
[2] See Philippians 2:13 NKJV.
[3] See Romans 5:17.
[4] See John 1:14; 2 Corinthians 5:14.

Jesus said that He did not come to invite the righteous to repentance, but the sinners.[5] Pray, therefore, this prayer with me if you desire to be born again. Pray it out loud since it is through confession that we confirm our salvation:

Lord, I confess to You that I am a sinner, and I ask You to save me from my sins. I confess that I cannot save myself and that only You can save me. I believe, Jesus, that You are the Son of God and the Savior of the world. I believe that You died on the cross to pay the price for my sins and that You rose the third day for my justification. I come to You, Father, in Jesus' name, and I ask You to save my soul and to make me new like Your Word promises. I repent of my sins, and I surrender my life to You. Come and live in my heart. Have Your way in me, for I belong to You. In Jesus' name, amen.

---

[5] See Luke 5:32.

CPSIA information can be obtained
at www.ICGtesting.com
Printed in the USA
BVHW041544290421
606135BV00002B/163

9 781603 835237